Twa Tribes

Scots among the Native Americans

Hugo Reid, Alexander Ross and Charles McKenzie

TOM BRYAN

NMS ENTERPRISES LIMITED

Published by NMS Publishing
a division of NMS Enterprises Limited
National Museums of Scotland
Chambers Street
Edinburgh EH1 1JF

© Tom Bryan and NMS Enterprises Limited 2003

With thanks to NMS Publishing Scots' Lives series editor: Iseabail Macleod

ISBN 1-901663-47-7

British Library Cataloguing in Publication Data
A catalogue record of this book
is available from the British Library.

ISBN 1 901663 47 7

Typeset in 11/14 pt Baskerville.
Design by NMS Publishing, NMS Enterprises Limited.
Cover design by Mark Blackadder.
Printed and bound in the United Kingdom by Bell & Bain Limited, Glasgow.

Contents

Acknowledgements

WITH special thanks to the staff of the National Library of Scotland for help in obtaining material on Alexander Ross; and Karen Clavelle of Winnipeg, Manitoba for providing invaluable assistance and information about Charles McKenzie. *A Scotch Paisano* by Susanna Bryant Dakin remains an excellent source book for the life and writings of Hugo Reid.

I would also like to thank the staff of the publishing division of NMS Enterprises Limited at the National Museums of Scotland for their patience and encouragement; and to all those persons who approach other cultures with tolerance and respect.

This book is dedicated to my son Michael and daughter Anna, who know about cultural bridges.

Preface

IT is difficult to write anything new about the relationship between European settlers and the Native peoples of the North American continent. Books and films have all had their say. It is also difficult not to create new stereotypes, even after the old ones have been challenged. Our language has changed. 'Indian' has given way to 'Native American' or 'First Nations people'; or more accurate renderings of tribal names like Lakota instead of Sioux, Eenou for Cree, and so on. 'Native American' is the current term in the United States of America, while 'First Nations people' prevails in Canada. Since much of my narrative concerns a time when Indians, trappers and explorers moved freely over the borders between what is now Canada, the United States of America and Mexico, I have retained the term 'Indian' in some contexts as one that is acceptable to the majority. Recently I heard a Lakota man state that 'Indian' was more acceptable to him than 'Native' or 'Native American'. I use the term as one of respect, knowing that it is not totally acceptable to everyone in this debate. Where possible I have tried to be specific as to tribe and peoples.

Often facts are enough to present a case. Some historians estimate that at the time of Christopher Columbus ten million people inhabited the land that is now the United States of America. By 1840 the numbers of Native peoples were thought to have been reduced to 400,000. The 1990 census in the USA listed just under two million persons as Native Americans, barely 0.79 per cent of the population. In Canada, First Nations peoples comprise just four per cent of the population. Yet until disease, warfare, famine and exploitation took their toll, the First Nations peoples on the continent lived for thousands of years as successful farmers, fishermen and nomadic hunters, speaking hundreds of separate languages, with a wide variety of religious and cultural beliefs.

Between 1607 and 1914 over 40 million Europeans came to America, to a land whose native population was already in decline. Scots made up a large number of those Europeans engaged in exploration and settlement of the country, and they gained vital knowledge from the Native people about dangerous animals they had never encountered before, including poisonous snakes and grizzly bears. They also learned ingenious methods of dealing with extremes of heat and cold, and other skills necessary for survival in their new land.

From even earlier times, Scots were notable among the pioneers of the New World. In his excellent book *Tam Blake and Company: The Story of the Scots in North America* (Edinburgh: Canongate Books, 1993) Jim Hewitson presents Tamas Blake, a Scot who explored the Grand Canyon in 1540 as one of Don Francisco Vasquez de Coronado's men. Coronado (1510-54), the 31-year-old Governor of New Spain, was an explorer and expedition leader whose search for gold took him deep into the American southwest. He set out from Mexico in 1540 to find the legendary 'Seven Cities of Cibola' in what is now New Mexico, where, according to the information of earlier Spanish explorers, the streets were paved with gold. The expedition wandered for thousands of miles, and despite enduring starvation and thirst managed to explore the present states of Arizona, New Mexico, Texas, Oklahoma and Kansas. Coronado did not find the legendary 'Cities' or expected hordes of gold and eventually returned to Spain disillusioned.

Blake was part of Coronado's side expedition under Garcia Lopez de Calderon which stumbled across the Grand Canyon. In this capacity he encountered the Native peoples of the southwest deserts. Members of the expedition presented them with one of the most valuable of gifts – the horse – which revolutionised Native society, particularly on the prairie and plains.

From Tam Blake to the present, people from all parts of Scotland have travelled out to all parts of the North American continent as explorers, trappers, scouts, settlers, missionaries and scientists. The purpose of this book is to highlight some individual experiences and to concentrate on those who made a special contribution to our understanding of that unique and often fascinating relationship between the 'twa tribes'.

Chapter 1
Native Peoples

HISTORY books tell us that the Native American culture evolved out of Asia over 30,000 years ago, from nomadic hunting over ice bridges. Each wandering group adapted to local conditions and became hunters, fishermen or farmers as their new environment demanded. Maize, squash, beans and tobacco were some of the crops common to these early peoples.

By the sixteenth century and the first incursions by the Spanish, the indigenous cultures were well-established and sophisticated. However, various colonial powers had different philosophies about the role of the Native peoples. The Spanish were interested in converting the Indians to Christianity, and acquiring their gold; the French were concerned with trade; while the British wanted colonies. The Colonial Government's Proclamation of 1763 may have ceded all lands west of the Appalachians to Native peoples, but by the nineteenth century it was epidemics, warfare and broken treaties that had come to define the relationship.

Later, Scottish settlers would have to decide where their individual consciences placed them in terms of an often shameful history of conflict between cultures. As people they were no better or worse than any other nationality, yet Scotland's own clan system, method of settlement, and historical mistreatment at the hands of a more dominant culture, could perhaps have allowed more sympathetic attitudes to prevail. There are certainly many examples of Scots assuming Indian ways and customs quite readily, some even becoming leaders within adopted tribes.

Scots

Scots have been present in North America as explorers, fishermen, fur trappers and indentured servants since the sixteenth and seventeenth centuries. However, the classic settlements were not established until after the Jacobite Rebellions and the Clearances of the eighteenth and nineteenth centuries respectively. By the mid-eighteenth century, contact between Scots and Native people was already commonplace and varied.

At the end of the seventeenth century, Scotland was in the grip of famine and overpopulation. The disastrous Darien Scheme, a bid to create a colony on the Isthmus of Panama to assist trade and emigration, drained Scotland's financial resources and brought about social and economic hardship. The Union of Parliaments in 1707 seemed almost inevitable.

In the build-up to the union with England and its aftermath, a period of deep unrest pervaded Scotland and riots began to break out in her major cities. Scotland's political independence had been surrendered, but with little relief from her long-standing economic problems. The new Parliament of Great Britain was not equal; England had little respect for a country and peoples considered backward and uncivilised.

The year 1715 saw the first Jacobite rising. Facing repression, loss of liberty, language, and a whole way of life, particularly among the clan-based Highland culture, there was a bid to reinstate the exiled House of Stuart. But when James Francis Edward Stuart, the pretender, arrived on the shores of Scotland, the rebellion was already a lost cause. Pro-government forces under the Duke of Argyll held the predominantly Highland Jacobites, and James left for France, leaving his supporters to their fate, which included some executions and forced transportation to the colonies (by 1729 many Jacobite refugees had begun to settle the coastal areas of North Carolina). More importantly, the aftermath of the rising hastened the decline of the clan system and its ancient culture.

But some Jacobites held firmly to their cause. The government had established a strong military presence in the Highlands and roads were now being built under the watchful eye of Major-General Wade, so it was not until 1745 that Charles Edward Stuart, son of James, arrived in Scotland to lead a rebellion. This time the clan chiefs recruited more by threat than loyalty. The Jacobites fought their way into England, but without popular support, and the small army dwindled as it returned to its final tragic stand at Culloden Moor on 16 April 1746. Once again Jacobites, including many Highlanders, were imprisoned, executed, or transported to the colonies as slaves or indentured servants. Their houses were burned, livestock driven south, and the clan system effectively destroyed. Some people left Scotland to escape reprisals; while others joined the growing number of Highland regiments of the British army.

New York and Pennsylvania in the north of America, and the Carolinas and Georgia in the south, became particular magnets for Highlanders, especially in the aftermath of 1745. Captain Lachlan Campbell from Islay, for example, settled over 80 families in New York in the country of the Iroquois, Huron, Mohawk and Delaware tribes. Further south, the main tribes were the Creek, Cherokee, Seminole, and Chickasaw.

As the colonial aspirations of Britain and France competed for North American hegemony, various shaky alliances were formed with the eastern indigenous tribes, creating a frontier warfare which particularly affected those Scots who came to America via Ulster and had pushed to the western boundaries of settlement. Scotland was an ideal recruitment ground for the British army.

By the mid-eighteenth century it was reported that Glasgow-based businesses were sending vessels to Maryland and Virginia as part of the great tobacco trade, bringing prosperity to Scots at home and abroad. Some suffered badly from the loss of trade brought about by the American Revolution. The 1776 war between Britain and her American colonies aided by their French and Indian allies, divided the Scottish community in two, with American victory in 1783 opening more of the country to emigration. British Loyalists were forced to settle in the Caribbean, or flee to Canada, resulting in population pressures on Canadian native tribes.

As the eighteenth century drew to a close, Scots at home were still restive. The year 1792 was to become known as *Bliadhna nan Caorach*, the 'Year of the Sheep'. The Clearances were underway. Highlanders with no security of tenure were being forced from the land by increasing rents to be replaced by Cheviot sheep. Families, even whole communities, moved to the Lowland cities in search of work, and from there to the colonies.

At the same time, encouraged by the achievements of the French Revolution, the more liberal middle-class and new working-class, created out of the 'golden age' of the Scottish Enlightenment, began a movement for reform. The government took action to quell acts of rebellion as they grew increasingly violent. Some Scots, like Alexander Wilson and Grant Thorburn, were branded as fugitives and were forced to leave the country.

In 1814 many Sutherland Scots settled the Red River Colony, a site near the present city of Winnipeg, Canada. Back home their families continued to suffer; industrialisation led to unemployment, while the population grew steadily. Scots weavers began to arrive in the Massachusetts and New

England weaving mills. The Highland potato famine of 1846, though not as widespread as that in Ireland, was yet another reason for emigration. The discovery of gold in California in 1848/9 enticed thousands of Europeans to the American west; and by 1862 the Homestead Act in America attracted impoverished Scots by the thousands.

The 1880s saw armed uprisings in the crofting townships of the Highlands resulting in victimisation and unemployment, and again Scots pursued emigration as a way to escape hardship. And as the century drew to a close, the great Scottish-based cattle-holding companies in America began to recruit managers and workers from their homeland. People from Dundee and Edinburgh figured heavily in this trade.

A climate of emigration had been created which brought Scots into ever-greater contact with North America's native population. Some of the most influential Scots were trappers, explorers, scientists and surveyors. The fur trade, in particular, attracted Gaelic-speaking Highlanders as well as young men from Shetland and Orkney, and probably provided the most contact between the 'twa tribes'. They had much in common: a strong sense of place and kinship, and the experience of displacement from their native land, and loss language at the hands of others.

Canada took the lead in establishing the fur trade with First Nations peoples, but America soon caught up and lured many trappers across the Border. Many of the most enduring contacts between Scots and Indians sprang from the fur trade because working conditions demanded a vital knowledge of local languages, customs, religion and culture. Gaels and Scots often had to travel into the interior alone or in small groups, and a trapper or scout's survival often depended on understanding the differences between Blackfeet and Crow, Lakota or Pawnee, for example. Stories are often recounted about one minor mispronunciation of a word that alerts a trapper to the fact that his hosts are not allies but potential enemies, enabling him to escape silently into the night.

It has been argued that many Scots excelled in this linguistic skill because of their own multi-lingual background in Gaelic, Scots and English; indeed there are many cases on record of Scots who acted as interpreters and translators. Robert Dickson of Dumfries, for example, was said to excel in various Lakota dialects; Hugh Monroe (or Munroe), on the other hand, was fluent in Blackfeet. Other interpreters and translators included Robert Stuart, John Stuart and Donald Mackenzie, many of whom were native Gaelic speakers. John MacLeod was a young Hudson's Bay clerk from Lochs in Lewis. He became an adept trader and explorer for the company in part because of his fluency in native languages. Sir George Simpson of the Hudson's Bay Company noted: 'MacLeod is an active well-behaved Man of tolerable Education. Speaks Cree, understands a little Chipewayan, is an excellent trader ....'. (George Simpson [1792-1860], a Highlander from Loch Broom, rose to become Governor in Chief of Hudson's Bay territories and was a key figure in its expansion.)

Indeed most Scots featured in this book understood the cultural and mercantile advantages of fluency in as many native languages as possible. William Dunbar from Elgin even conducted a special study of the Indian sign languages in his adopted state of Mississippi.

However, it would be misleading to believe that all contact between Scots and First Nations people were in the arena of trading or commerce. Although there were economic advantages to be gained for those learning local languages and dialects, many Scots had other objectives in mind.

Medical men and scientists formed a key part of the emigration movement. John Rae (1813-93) was an Orkney man who was employed as a surgeon in the Hudson's Bay Company, but who also spent much of his time studying the flora and fauna of Canada. He surveyed a great extent of the wilderness, charting over 700 miles of previously unknown coastline.

Rae was an open and tolerant man who paid tribute to the native people of the north who taught him his wilderness craft. He learned to travel swiftly and effectively by living simply, and it is reported that he once walked 40 miles on snowshoes just to keep a dinner date. A famous portrait exists of Rae attired in the full dress of the Cree Indians; however, like other Europeans who adopted a sympathetic lifestyle, he was criticised by some for 'going native'. Nonetheless, Rae exemplified the need for white people to learn from those who knew the country best, and his writings express genuine admiration for indigenous culture.

Samuel Muir (1789-1832) was also a surgeon. Born in Washington DC, the son of the Reverend James Muir of Cumnock, Ayrshire. Muir was serving as an army surgeon when he fell in love with the daughter of the chief of the Sac-Fox tribe. He married into the tribe, adopting their customs and language, and became an important tribal leader.

Men of religion also played their part. Scotland sent many missionaries to the far corners of the globe, and North America was no exception.

Because of the French power base, many of the first missionaries to work with the Native peoples were Catholic and Jesuit, but more and more Scottish men of religion arrived. John Gibson, like Muir, was born of Scottish parents in America and first worked with the Creeks in Arkansas, while his wife ran the local school. Gibson was the first to capture the Cherokee language as written script. Although the American government was not supportive of Gibson's efforts, he went on to carry out similar work with other tribes in the north and west.

* * *

This account of the 'twa tribes' is not intended as a patronising hymn to Scottish tolerance and fair play. That account would not be true. Tales of Scottish individuals involved in acts of killing and massacre in North America would fill a book in itself, and not a particularly honourable one. A list of those who fought against Indians on the frontier, for example, would include Scots like Thomas McGregor, Ranald Slidell Mackenzie and Andy Hall, to name but a few (see Appendix II, page 80). There were also those like Sir Alexander Cuming of Aberdeenshire who, through deceitful means, persuaded Indian people to crown him 'Emperor of the Cherokee' and 'Crown King of Tennessee'.

What is remarkable, however, is the number of genuine chiefs and tribal leaders who had Scottish connections. The names Alexander McGillivray, John Ross and Willie McIntosh spring to mind, all famous leaders of their people, and all descended from Highlanders. Flett, another example, is a common surname among the leaders of the Manitoba Cree Nation, yet it is also a surname specific to the Orkney Islands.

Other Scots, though much less elevated, married into native clans which gave them great standing as tribal advisors. Robert Dickson, Hugh Monroe, Samuel Muir, and Lachlan McGillivray, for example, married daughters of chiefs and assumed great influence in tribal council.

Common Threads

Despite the thousands of Scots who had contact with the Native peoples of North America, there is a rationale for the particular selection of Hugo

Reid (1810-52), Alexander Ross (1783-1856) and Charles McKenzie (1778-1855) as suitable examples for this book on 'twa tribes'. It is tempting to try to portray these three as men who fought for the rights of Native peoples, entirely escaping the prejudices and institutionalised racism of their time. The truth is they could not and did not quite escape these notions, being well aware of prevailing perceptions of the 'white man's burden' and the responsibility to bring 'civilisation' to the 'savages'. Ross, Reid and McKenzie grew up within the dominant Protestant culture of the age which sent missionaries around the world to do just that.

Nonetheless, Reid, Ross and McKenzie came independently to the conclusion that the Native peoples were sophisticated and intelligent; and that is why the legacy of their writings is so valuable.

Let us look at what Reid, Ross and McKenzie had in common. In broad terms these three men from Scotland crossed a wide ocean and adopted a new way of life. And in doing so they gradually altered their opinions and challenged their own prejudices. They may not have left Scotland with the sole intention of interacting with native cultures. However, although variously employed (Reid as a businessman, trader and merchant, Ross as a schoolteacher, and McKenzie as a clerk), they quickly became fascinated with the languages and customs of the people they worked among, and through time adopted more sympathetic attitudes.

Reid, Ross and McKenzie all left Scotland never to return. They married native women, remaining serious about their commitment to their wives. They also fought for the rights of their partners and children, challenging the deeply-held prejudices their own mixed-blood offspring would later encounter. And although none had previous knowledge of languages or customs foreign to his own, all three were to learn native languages and leave important written legacies about the religion, law, work and ways of life of their respective adopted peoples – all valuable contributions to today's understanding of how diverse cultures collide, adapt or dovetail.

Scots in particular might feel that their own strong cultural sense, along with a troubled history of displacement and emigration, should result in tolerance and mutual respect for different cultures. Perhaps that is the most important common thread, the one that ties the modern-day reader to three remarkable individuals who, through their work with Native peoples, managed to question if not escape entirely the prejudices of their own time.

Chapter 2
The Fur Trade

The Canadian Fur Trade

ALTHOUGH Scottish contact with First Nations peoples occurred in a variety of ways, exploration, trade and cultural assimilation came principally through the fur trade in Canada, filtering into America when the latter nation's fur trade developed centuries later.

The Canadian fur trade began in the sixteenth century. As early as the 1520s, fishermen from Northern Europe could be found off the eastern coast of Canada, on the world's prime cod fishing grounds, the Grand Banks off Newfoundland and up the St Lawrence River. There was a vast European market for dried cod at the time and the fishermen took their catch on shore to dry, a process which could last for several weeks, depending on the weather. As they waited they began to trade with the local tribes, offering them metal goods and utensils such as axes, knives, iron tools, kettles, blankets and cloth goods. In return the Indians traded meat and furs. Furs became very profitable and the demand for felt hats in Europe proved lucrative to those early sixteenth-century fishermen-cum-fur-traders. Canadian beaver provided the soft underfur for hat felt; its strong barbs gave it an almost self-adhesive effect, like velcro.

Those early trading experiences helped the fur industry to develop, once the first important tribal contacts had been established. The French developed the trade in eastern Canada and Quebec, while the Dutch expanded their business up the Hudson River. By the 1620s the French had developed a strong fur-trapping and fur-trading industry and had gained a useful knowledge of Indian customs and languages. When British and French colonial interests began to collide, the latter had already established control over the waterways and extensive kinship with the tribes, with many French trappers married to native women.

By the late seventeenth century, British interests in the fur trade resulted in the creation of the Hudson's Bay Company.

The Hudson's Bay Company

The founding of the Hudson's Bay Company in May 1670 was to have profound effects on both Scots and Early Nations peoples. From the beginning Orcadians, Shetlanders and Gaelic-speaking Highlanders worked for this company, whose monolithic structure resembled a military organisation. The early years involved fierce competition with French interests, but gradually Hudson's Bay began to emerge as the real power in Canadian politics and expansion, its trademark being the establishment of trading posts at the mouths of rivers leading into the Bay. And just as the company rose to challenge French hegemony in the New World, so other companies rose to challenge Hudson's Bay.

The North West Company

The western rival to Hudson's Bay, the North West Company, proved to be a great magnet for Gaelic-speaking Scots. Successful clerks and trappers would often bring their kinfolk over from Scotland, and families such as MacTavish, Mackenzie and Farquharson became dynasties in the North American fur trade. In 1821, when the two great rivals merged, the majority of the new company's officers were Highlanders from the old North West Company.

From its inception in 1784 until its merger with Hudson's Bay, the North West Company proved much more successful at relations with Early Nations peoples and permitted all ranks to intermarry with local women, thus establishing the blood-ties to the western tribes which were lacking in Hudson's Bay. This policy resulted in many Scots adopting Indian culture and customs. Not only did the fur trade have a profound effect on the relationship between Early Nations and European peoples, but in Canada at least it also created a society which blended both worlds through marriage and adaptation. It is from this blending that some of the most fascinating stories emerged, forming the basis of popular culture. The heroic adventures depicted in books, magazines, children's annuals and songs, and more recently films, are somewhat romanticised, but their roots are firmly planted in the realities of the fur-trapping way of life.

By the nature of the business, trappers had to work in Indian country, and so they traded with them and learned about local conditions. Any of these men seeking the stability of family life would have had to do so with local women, since the era of fur trapping preceded any later settlement of European women west of the Great Divide. The three men featured in this book (and many more included in Appendix II, page 80) took this particular route, marrying local women, achieving high status within their adopted tribes, and learning the languages, customs and skills of their new family and friends.

The history of the Canadian fur trade is grounded in the history of the early French trappers, the *voyageurs*, the expansion of Hudson's Bay and North West companies, their rivalry and eventual merger. However it should not be forgotten that the borders and loyalties between British Canada and the United States were not as fixed as they are today. Trappers freely crossed over that boundary and offered their skills to the highest bidder, American or Canadian. Scots like Kenneth Mackenzie, Donald Mackenzie, Robert Dickson and others began their careers in Canada, but became leading figures in the business and politics of neighbouring America. Many were attracted to more favourable pay and conditions south of the Border and it is worth taking a look at the American trade before continuing with the accounts of Reid, Ross and McKenzie.

The American Fur Trade

Unlike Canada the American fur trade was better suited to individuals and men working in small teams. As it was not corporate in structure it is not surprising to find that colourful individuals formed its backbone, including many Scottish and Irish immigrants. Men like John Colter, Jedediah Smith, Broken Hand Fitzpatrick and the Sublette brothers, for example, became part of the legend which survives in poetry and song to this day.

The Perthshire landowner William Drummond Stewart ('The Buckskin Baronet') was so enamoured of the fur-trapping myth that he brought buffalo, scouts and Indians back to Scotland to enrich the life of his estate. Stewart was an aristocrat and soldier who had lived for almost eight years in the Rocky Mountains in the company of frontiersmen and scouts and he was highly regarded in the west for his bravery and skill. When he retired to Perthshire, Stewart had a collection of mementos of his life in America, including paintings by the renowned artist Alfred Jacob

Miller (1810-74) who recorded many scenes of the lives of Indians and trappers.

The humble beaver was mainly responsible for the decades of fur-trapping adventure, mainly 1810-30, in the western mountains. The rodent's underfur was considered ideal for the fashion industry in Europe and over 100,000 beaver pelts were used by hatters each year to supply their market. However the pelts were obtained at great peril. Men drowned, died of disease, starvation and exposure, and fell prey to marauding bands of Indians, all in the attempt to trap the animal. The Blackfeet in particular, a tribe of the Algonquin Indians, did not tolerate Europeans encroaching on their lands.

Many men were inspired to go west on hearing reports of the Lewis and Clark Expedition of 1804-06. Captains Meriwether Lewis and William Clark led the expedition from St Louis to the Pacific Ocean. Their descriptions of the wildlife and natural landscape of the Rocky Mountains and far west destroyed the myth of 'The Great American Desert' and painted a compelling picture of a land teeming with fish and game, a land full of natural wonders and colourful peoples. Manuel Lisa, for example, on the strength of the reports, founded the Missouri Fur Company, building forts deep into Indian country. Lisa was the first to introduce commercial fur trading to the western mountains in 1807, using one John Colter as his guide. The first trading post was built at the mouth of the Big Horn River.

However, for the purposes of this book and its theme of Scottish relations with Native peoples, it is worth looking at the two most important American fur companies – the Rocky Mountain Fur Company and the American Fur Company (with its offshoot, the Pacific Fur Company) – as many Scots worked for these outfits, having first learned their trade in Canada with either the North West or Hudson's Bay companies.

The American Fur Company

The German-born New Yorker, John Jacob Astor, founded the American Fur Company in 1808 and its subsidiary, the Pacific Fur Company, in 1810. Astor had been content for many years to base his business by the Missouri River and its tributaries, but its westward expansion, to Astoria at the mouth of the Columbia River, part of the Oregon Territory at that time (now Washington State), brought his business into conflict with some of its greatest rivals.

Astor's vast wealth meant that his fur companies could afford to lose money for several years, while at the same time poaching leading fur traders from other companies, including Rocky Mountain Fur. By the mid-1820s Astor's associate, the Greenock-born Ramsay Crooks, began to make incursions into the Rocky Mountains, and by 1827 American Fur had bought out Missouri Fur and Columbia Fur, smaller independent companies. Ordering his recruits Pierre Chouteau and Kenneth Mackenzie 'to wipe out the opposition' ('*écraser toute opposition,*' in Chouteau's words), these highly-experienced traders soon extended Astor's eastern monopoly into the west. Mackenzie's technique involved handing out weapons freely to his Indian allies and paying outrageous prices for pelts in order to wipe out the opposition. By such methods American Fur had secured the difficult Blackfeet trade by 1830.

Astor then extended the company's line of forts into the Upper Missouri, consolidating most of the American fur business. By the time he sold out his interest in the business in 1834, its combined activities had made it the largest commercial operation in America.

The Rocky Mountain Fur Company

This historic company was founded in 1822 by two St Louis merchants, General Ashley and Andrew Henry. They came up with the novel idea that instead of using forts, which were easy to attack and a provocation to Native peoples, trappers would bring all the furs to a pre-agreed rendezvous point. In addition the company encouraged the free trapper, working alone and living off the land, to sell his pelts to the highest bidder. This rugged individualism was to attract many Scots who had grown tired of the bureaucratic paternalism of the Canadian companies.

Out of desire or necessity, the lonely way of life of the trapper meant that these individuals had to adopt Indian ways or die. Most took Indian wives and wintered with their people, learning the language and culture and sometimes assisting them in hunting or fighting enemies. Scots such as Hugh Monroe, Alexander Ross and Kenneth Mackenzie are known to have pursued this way of life.

It is almost easy to understand the attraction of the fur-trapping way of life to a young Scot from Orkney, Shetland, the Hebrides or the Highlands. He would no doubt be used to cold, privation and physical danger. The pay was good, and his strength, cultivated on a croft or boat in his homeland, would be to his advantage.

The Native peoples might have responded well to the treatment they received from these Scots. A Gaelic speaker learning English would almost certainly be able to relate to Indians learning English or French. Many tribes used a clan system not dissimilar to the Scots, and the Indian loyalty to a chief or tribe would be a familiar notion. It is not surprising therefore that many Highlanders found Indian ways and customs almost preferable to European ways in the settlements.

The vocabulary any young Scot picked up in the western mountains illustrated their relationship with the local people, for good or bad. To 'black your face against', for example, meant to be at odds with someone. To 'count coup' was to do a brave deed, fur-trappers' slang for doing something reckless. Usually this had to include an element of surprise, and be against the odds – like killing someone in hand-to-hand combat, taking a scalp, stealing a horse from your enemy, or making a fool of your rival with the knowledge that you could have done him even greater harm had you so wished. It also meant to recite your brave deed in a public place, to the shame or embarrassment of your enemy or rival. Striking someone with a 'coup stick' was a bold thing to do, especially if you rode into an enemy camp to do so and remained unharmed. And to have 'the har o the bar' ('the hair of the bear') was the supreme measure of bravery, coming from the Indian belief that eating the hair of the grizzly bear would make you braver.

In his excellent book *Give Your Heart to the Hawks* (New York: Avon, 1976), historian Winfred Blevins comments on the natural assimilation of trappers into Indian ways and the fur-trappers' discomfort when they saw settlers coming west in ever greater numbers; for like the Indians, their own way of life depended on plentiful buffalo and other game:

> *And the attitude of the mountain men toward the Indians evolved from calculated strategy into felt identification. Between 1822, when the Ashley men first went West, and 1843, when the first hordes of emigrants came, the trappers in a way became Indians themselves. They dressed like Indians, adopted some of the values of Indians, learned Indian languages, married (sometimes permanently) into Indian tribes, and came to*

believe in Indian religion, which was more relevant to their circumstances than the allegories of Moses and Christ. When the first missionaries came, they saw instantly that the mountain men were more Indian than white. By the 1840s, to say 'I took ee for an Injun' was a compliment to a trapper, though an abhorrence to an emigrant. The emigrants defeated the mountain men as surely as they defeated the Indians.

Since the fur trade was linked to the precarious European fashion for beaver hats, the American fur trade all but collapsed when, by 1840, silk replaced fur. Although historically brief, the fur-trapping saga was unique in the history of the west, coming before settlement and the despoliation of the buffalo herds and the Indian way of life.

'Company men'

A few selected thumbnail biographies (see also page 80) may help to illustrate the complex relationships between the various fur companies in Canada and the United States as men were recruited from one company to another on the promise of higher wages and better prices. Hudson's Bay may have enjoyed a near monopoly until challenged by North West in 1821, but merger between the two in turn spawned further competition from the Americans.

Two typical Hudson's Bay 'company' men were Robert Campbell and Hugh Monroe. Campbell was born in Glen Lyon, Perthshire in 1808 and died in Winnipeg, Manitoba in 1894. He was persuaded to join Hudson's Bay by his cousin, James McMillan, a chief trader with the company, and became an expert hunter and trapper. He was also a capable leader. During one expedition he boiled up his snowshoes to make an edible paste to keep his men alive; another time he travelled through an entire Canadian winter with no food, water or clothing, having been robbed and stripped. It is also told how he made a journey of 3000 miles on snow-shoes. Campbell lived to a ripe old age in the settlements, something he attributed to his austere religion and a habit of taking a morning dip in ice-choked rivers. Despite his achievements, however, he eschewed fame or recognition, and instead built up a reputation for his sermons, favouring prophetic passages from the Book of Joshua. Campbell exemplifies the old-fashioned approach Hudson's encouraged.

Hugh Monroe (or Munroe) (1798-1892) was another long-lived Hudson's veteran. Less is known about his life in Scotland, but we know that he arrived in western Canada in 1814 and revealed a great aptitude for company life. Monroe absorbed native languages and made friends with the Blackfeet, a notoriously difficult achievement. Monroe married Sinopa, Chief Lone Walker's daughter, and lived with the Blackfeet Nation for most of his long and fascinating life. He was commissioned to explore and map much of the Blackfeet country in what is now southern Alberta and northern Montana, and at his death was buried on the Two Medicine River in Alberta.

Kenneth Mackenzie was another type of trapper, cutting his teeth in the Canadian fur trade with the more progressive North West but making his fortune in the American fur trade. Mackenzie was born in 1797 in Ross-shire. In 1822 he arrived in St Louis, then the pivotal city in the American fur trade. All expeditions started out from there and travelled up the Mississippi and Missouri into the heart of trapping country. Mackenzie, nicknamed 'King of the Missouri' or 'Emperor of the West', was a colourful and controversial character and he fully enjoyed this role. His base at Fort Union was provisioned with the best brandy and wine, he dressed in European fashion, and resorted to any means to erase his opposition. Later, he speculated in land and railways, making a vast fortune in both. Far removed from 'company man' Robert Campbell, Mackenzie represented a breed of independent trapper-cum-entrepreneur that Hudson's Bay would never encourage.

Robert Stuart was similar to Mackenzie in that he learned his trade in Canada but took his skills to America where he was made head of the American Fur's operations in the Great Lakes area. Stuart was born in Callander, Perthshire in 1785 and died in Chicago in 1848. His grandfather was a great rival of the famous Rob Roy McGregor. Stuart worked as a fisherman off Labrador before taking up trapping. Said to be only the third man ever to cross the Continent in a canoe, he made a number of epic journeys including one from the Pacific Coast all the way to St Louis with the aforementioned associate of Astor, Ramsay Crooks. In later life he became Superintendent for Indian Affairs in Michigan, a post awarded because of his knowledge of native languages and customs. The great American novelist Washington Irving left us a description of Stuart in his history of John Jacob Astor's fur post at Astoria on the Columbia River.

Stuart was an easy soul and of a social disposition. He had seen life in Canada and on the coast of Labrador; had been a fur trader in the former and a fisherman on the latter, and in the course of his experiences had made various expeditions with voyageurs. *He was accustomed, therefore, to the familiarity which prevails between that class and their superiors, and the gossipings which take place among them when seated round a fire at their encampments. Stuart was never so happy as when he could seat himself on the deck with a number of these men around him in camping style, smoke together, passing the pipe from mouth to mouth, after the manner of the Indians; sing old Canadian boat songs, and tell stories about their hardships and adventures, in the course of which he rivalled Sinbad in his long tales of the sea, about his fishing exploits off Labrador.*

(Washington Irving, *Astoria*, Philadelphia, 1836)

Robert Dickson, a native of Dumfries, was born in 1765 and died in Michigan in 1823. His story embodies the fur-trapping way of life. Dickson began trapping in Canada and established his own fur company. An influential figure with the Sioux, he married a chief's daughter called To-to-Win. During the War of 1812, the American extension of the Napoleonic Wars 1812-1814, Dickson fought on the side of the British against the Americans and their French allies. He was known to have harboured a unique vision of an industrial settlement of white people and Indians at the site of Grand Forks in what is now North Dakota, a vision based on the just principles of trade and co-operation. Dickson played a major role in the settlement of Wisconsin and Michigan and his knowledge of native customs and languages led to his appointment as Indian Agent for the Great Lakes region.

These are just some outstanding examples of that blend of vision and practicality which Scots, both Highland and Lowland, brought to their North American experience, a blend that is evident in the story of Hugo Reid, our first featured Scot among the Native Americans.

Chapter 3
Hugo Reid:
'The Scotch Paisano'

THE story of Hugo Reid, 'the Scotch Paisano' or countryman, has all the elements of fiction. A son of small-town Scottish shopkeepers, he studied hard and attended Cambridge University. At the age of 18, jilted by his lover Victoria, he shipped out to South America where he wandered restlessly for six years, having many adventures before settling in Mexico, where he became a citizen, and then in that part of the country which was to become the state of California.

Reid was involved in various intrigues and was charged with smuggling while trading in the Sandwich Islands (modern-day Hawaii). Smuggling in Reid's day meant simply an evasion of taxes or duties, and he was eventually cleared of the charges and able to continue trading.

In California Reid fell in love again, this time with a married Indian woman with four children, whose husband had died of smallpox. Converting to Catholicism, as required by law, Reid was able to marry the widow and to obtain land.

It was Reid's observations of his wife's people, and of the oppressed Californian Indians in general, that was to awaken the conscience of an entire nation, and his contribution to human rights in America, despite his premature death at the age of 42, is still considered of great importance.

Early Life

On his application for marriage on 30 July 1837 Reid stated that he was *'Perfecto Hugo Reid, native of great Britain, legitimate son of Charles Reid and Essex Milchin, natives of Scotland in the County of Renfrew ...'*.

Reid, whose life was influenced so much by the Pacific Ocean, was born in Cardross, Dunbartonshire in 1810. The Celtic name for Cardross, meaning 'wood point', describes its location, three and a half miles north-west of Dumbarton. Cardross combined inland farming with occupations associated with the life of the River Clyde, mirroring Reid's later experience as a rancher, and as a maritime trader in locations as far away as Hawaii.

When the young Reid was jilted, the experience prompted him to leave Scotland to seek his fortune in South America. There he learned several languages fluently, including Spanish, and by 1832 became a merchant in the capital of Sonora, Hermosillo, in Northern Mexico.

A visit to what is now Los Angeles convinced Reid that this was where his future and fortune might lie, especially after the gold boom in Mexico had died down, a boom that provided him with enough money to make his move north. In 1834 Reid set himself up as a trader in Los Angeles, dealing in silk, muslin, dry goods, tea and coffee, spices, gold and silver, and even Chinese fireworks. He then made the acquaintance of Dona Victoria, a married full-blooded Indian of the Gabrielenosa, a powerful local tribe who had been subjugated by the Spanish and their ancient tribal lands confiscated. Dona Victoria had been removed from her own people and brought up in the Spanish mission. She later married a man 28 years her senior and bore him four children.

Meanwhile Reid found himself implicated in a revolution against the Governor of Spanish California, Figueroa, for which he was fined but eventually pardoned of any wrongdoing. His business failed, however, and he returned to Hermosillo in 1836 when Texas and Mexico were at war. The part of Mexico known as Texas rebelled against Mexican rule, leading to the famous siege of the Alamo. A decade later, America and Mexico went to war (1846-48) over the annexation of Texas by America in 1845. America was to gain New Mexico and Texas from the conflict. Reid followed the events with interest since it affected him directly. Formerly a subject of Mexico, he now became an American.

Reid settled into a new job as a teacher of English, arithmetic, writing and geography and in his spare time began translating popular songs from English into Spanish, including the well-known 'Home Sweet Home'. After a year of teaching Reid learned that Dona Victoria's husband had died of smallpox, so he left Northern Mexico and returned to California to court the widow who ironically shared the same name as the young woman who had hastened his flight from Scotland in the first place.

Marriage to any local woman, especially a widow, was a complicated business. Reid had to convert to Catholicism, undergo an exhaustive investigation into his marriage credentials, and supply character witnesses. The record of his oath-taking upon application, as recorded by the Reverend Fray Tomas Eleuterio de Estenaga, clergyman in the former mission of San Gabriel Archangel, is outlined below:

> *Immediately after, there appeared at my request the above-mentioned Perfecto Hugo Reid, who took the oath, in the name of Our Lord and the Holy Cross, to answer truthfully all questions put to him, in the presence of assisting witnesses.*
>
> 1. *Question: What is your name, your parents' names, your age, and present condition.*
>   *He answered that his name was Perfecto Hugo Reid, legitimate son of Charles Reid and Essex Milchin, natives of Scotland in the County of Renfrew, resident of Our Lady of the Angels; his age, 27 years old, single.*
> 2. *If he is pledged to marry any other woman than the above-mentioned Bartolomea* [Dona Victoria's family name].
>   *He answered, no.*
> 3. *Question: Whether any force is being exerted on him to marry.*
>   *He answered, no.*
> 4. *Question: If he is a blood relation of the above-mentioned Bartolomea or connected with her by affinity or some other spiritual bond.*
>   *He answered, no.*
> 5. *Question: If he has taken a vow of chastity, of a religious or any other nature, and if there exist any other obstacles.*
>   *He answered, no.*
>
> *The foregoing having been read by him and confirmed by him, he signed together with me, that it be recorded, as well as of the assisting witnesses, the second placing his mark, not knowing how to write.*
>
> *Perfecto Hugo Reid, Santiago Suner, Fray Tomas Estenaga, Nicolas Diaz*

Permission was granted to marry the widow on 20 August 1837 by Fray Narciso Duran, Ecclesiastical Judge of Alta California.

It was rare for Mexican authorities to allow land grants to Indians like Reid's wife, but she laid claim to, and was eventually granted, two ranches which Reid set out to improve. The property at San Gabriel was called *Uva Espina* ('The Gooseberry'). Reid modified the rather dilapidated homestead structurally many times to ease Dona Victoria's fears about living in it. She harboured very real concerns about earthquakes in the area.

Reid agreed to educate Dona Victoria's children himself rather than entrust them to the mission since Dona Victoria had endured such misery in their care, a combination of the worst features of an orphanage and borstal. Missions were the political and religious focal point of life in Spanish California. Local people, including children, became involved with the missions in many ways from early schooling to a variety of domestic arrangements. Children worked long hours at hard tasks at the whim of local clerics; and Indian children were at particular risk of exploitation by priests and mission staff alike.

In 1839 Reid was elected to the Los Angeles city council, the beginning of his civic involvement. In this year he was also pursuing his wife's claim to her second ranch, despite clear prejudice against Indians holding land in California. He took the case directly to the Governor, a radical move, and won.

Although Reid's many preserved letters reveal his obvious pleasure in his family and ranch, the old wanderlust was never far away. By 1842 he appeared to be in business once more, trading up and down the coast in his ship *Esmeralda*, sailing as far away as Hawaii and spending up to six months at sea. Eventually high port duties on goods made maritime trading impractical. This time, on returning to his ranch, he was forced to sell land and livestock to pay off the shipping debts he had accrued, and he embarked upon some sound schemes for wine-making and citrus-growing, rightly predicting that these enterprises would flourish in the favourable climate.

When not at sea, Reid's work in the local area made him so popular that he was made Justice of the Peace, the highest elected office. He acquired such a favourable reputation for fair-dealing with the local Indians that the tribes insisted *he* baptise their children instead of the local priest.

Some of the local Indians were still engaged in acts of rebellion at that time, attacking outlying ranches and missions. Reid applied to various authorities to calm the situation by relaxing certain codes and attitudes, offering Indians more than the passive slavery they were used to. Reid's public utterances made it clear that he sympathised with the Indians and understood their poverty and subjugation. It was also apparent that he was highly sceptical of their conversion to Christianity by the Spanish and the unfair methods used to obtain that conversion.

In the early 1840s Reid bought the debt-ridden local mission and began to reform the treatment of the Indians, while trying to maintain basic law and order by dealing with marauding bands from elsewhere. Reid was fairly certain that public sentiment would result in a backlash against all tribes unless the lawless few were brought to justice, and he was put under immense pressure by local authorities and landowners alike, and clearly torn between peoples.

In his role as Justice of the Peace, Reid was compelled to authorise an expedition of soldiers into the mountains to quell the individuals acting outwith authority. It was not without incident. On one occasion, it is noted, they had to lasso eleven grizzly bears before they could proceed with the task in hand.

Personal debts, Indian uprisings and political squabbles were just the tip of the iceberg for Reid at that time. Part of the fascination about the man is that he lived during some of the great historical events of his day, such as the war with Mexico, the California Gold Rush (1848/9 to mid 1850s), and the creation of California as an American state in 1851. Up to that time California had been part of Spanish Catholic Mexico and Reid was originally a Mexican citizen by naturalisation.

He was well aware of impending war. In 1836 he had followed the separation of Texas from Mexico avidly and assumed the same situation could happen to California. To complicate matters, British agents were active in California trying to induce the region to separate from Mexico, to resist American encroachment, and to come under a British protectorate. Reid, a Scot by birth but now a Spanish-speaking Catholic Mexican, had several American friends and business partners and played a number of diplomatic roles, trying to opt for reason and peace. However, Reid had other things to worry about. When his mission and land were confiscated without compensation by the United States government, leaving him deeply in debt by 1849, Reid and many others looked to the Californian Gold Rush with great interest.

The Californian Gold Rush began when one James Marshall spotted a glint of the precious metal while building a sawmill at Sutter's Fort, Sierra Nevada. Four months later a whole bottle of gold dust was panned by the man who tended the store at Sutterville. The Rush was unstoppable and set to change both the political and social history of California for all time.

Reid knew all about gold. As a businessman in Hermosillo when the precious metal was discovered there, he understood the boom-and-bust mentality well. But he was also aware of the hazards of mining; and understood that the great influx of immigrants to California had wider implications.

Reid managed to achieve some prosperity from the Californian Gold Rush as a partner in a business supplying essential goods to miners; and in this capacity he was to become a witness and chronicler of events in northern California during that time.

Reid was given the honour of being a member of the first constitutional convention for California and was especially concerned by the lawlessness of the various vigilante groups patrolling the streets of San Francisco. He realised, as did many astute politicians, that admission to the United States as soon as possible would give Californians the much-needed protection of written law. Reid served on two important committees: one to establish the precise boundaries, the other to take a census. Partly at his insistence, other issues discussed included the civil rights of women, Indians and freed former slaves. When California finally achieved statehood, the last day of the first-ever legislative session was devoted to 'The Indian Question', largely because of Reid. However, although California had gone further than Spain or Mexico in granting certain rights, Reid was still not satisfied.

With statehood achieved, Reid returned home to southern California to try to avert his own impending financial ruin. His health, which had never been very good – he had suffered from breathlessness and lung complaints for many years – was beginning to show marked deterioration. He was only 40 years old.

Once home, Reid decided to pursue a belated promise. Many years before he had told Dona Victoria that he would do anything he could to help her people vindicate their pride, and it was at this otherwise low ebb in his life that he began to gather material on the Native peoples of California. He relied heavily on his wife's memory and experience, but also began to interview some of the older Indians in the area.

In the spring of 1851 Reid seemed to vanish from the planet. His wife did not know of his whereabouts, nor any of his close friends. Later he quietly reappeared, saying that he had gone into retreat to finish his research on Indian culture and behaviour. On 21 February 1852 the *Los*

Angeles Star announced that the editor had received 'a series of articles upon the manners, customs, *et cetera*, of the Indians, from the pen of Hugo Reid, Esq., a gentleman well conversant with the subject'. In the form of letters to the newspaper, Reid had produced his greatest work.

It is ironic that Reid had barely finished his writings when tuberculosis finally overcame him. He died on 12 December 1852 and was buried in the Old Catholic Cemetery in the pueblo of San Gabriel. Tragically Dona Victoria eventually succumbed to smallpox, which also claimed their children. She died in December 1868.

A sailor, businessman, householder, farmer, and legislator, Hugo Reid was also one of Mexico's and California's pioneers and leading citizens. From Scotland his travels took him via South America to the far reaches of the Pacific Ocean. During his lifetime he survived Indian attack, smallpox, violent earthquakes. Yet, most remarkable of all, despite constant poor health he survived long enough to leave a legacy of compassion – the extant writings of a person whose name was to become synonymous with Indian rights.

* * *

Hugo Reid – *The Writings*

Hugo Reid could write in at least three languages – English, Spanish and French – and could speak and understand several Indian languages as well. He was engaged at a decent salary by William Rand, editor of the *Los Angeles Star*, as San Gabriel correspondent for the paper. Reid's letters, each written on a different topic, appeared every Saturday in the paper. The letters themselves, from their first appearance on 21 February 1852, have been preserved in California's Bancroft Library and are reproduced in the excellent standard work on Hugo Reid's life, *A Scotch Paisano: Hugo Reid's Life in California, 1832-1852* by Susanna Bryant Dakin.

LETTER 1 – Lodges

In this letter Reid details the tribes (lodges, *rancherias*) in their own language and in the anglicised version. For example, the Los Angeles Indians are

Yang-na, the San Gabriel are *Sibag-na*, and so on. He comments, 'that these names formerly had a signification there can be no doubt of. But even the oldest now alive confess themselves ignorant of their meaning.'

Reid makes a significant point about the naming of tribes. Europeans, in this case Spanish missionaries, misunderstood local words and mis-applied them thereafter, resulting in confusion about language, culture and custom. It is interesting to speculate whether Reid understood how much Gaelic Scotland had suffered from the same confusion.

LETTER 2 – Language

This letter proved to be a revelation to scholars. Reid was a fine linguist, and his reputation as a strong singer and mimic supports his sensitivity to sound and language. Reid claims that most of the local Los Angeles tribes, being related by blood and marriage, were at first very alike and spoke a similar language, with very marked local accents, perhaps in the same way that different dialects of the Scots language appear similar. He lists numbers, words and phrases and provides a chart on the formation of verbs. Possibly for the first time a European was taking time and care to discover unique features in the Indian vocabulary. Says Reid:

> *Their language is simple, rich, and abounding in compound expressive terms. Although they have words denoting to desire, to like, to possess, to regard, to have an affection for, and to esteem; yet they have no word to express love. At the same time, they have many phrases for which we have no equivalent.*

It is clear that, even by 1850, Reid was witnessing the death of an ancient culture:

> *Their language has deteriorated so much since the* [Spanish] *conquest, that the present generation barely comprehend a part of what one of the 'old standards' say, when they speak the original tongue.*

[The Spanish conquest began with the subjugation of the Aztec people by Cortés in 1571, ending with the Mexican Colonial revolt in 1810.]

LETTER 3 – Government, Laws and Punishments

This letter sparked a great deal of interest when it first appeared because it exhibited an 'insider's' knowledge, probably Dona Victoria. Reid notes that tribal 'laws were made as required' and states that robbery, murder and incest were rare, the latter two punishable by death. (The accused was killed with a volley of arrows.) Disputes were heard by chiefs and sometimes decided by a neutral third party. Probably the most curious custom concerned infidelity. In some cases the cuckolded husband informed the lover that he could keep his wife, provided the cuckold could have the lover's wife in return. Reid felt that the local laws were governed by common sense and a keen insight into human psychology, and he constantly emphasised the natural wisdom of native cultures that Californians had hitherto despised or misunderstood.

LETTER 4 – Religion and Creed

This is an incredible letter. The parallels of Native beliefs to Christianity are uncanny: creation out of chaos, and a man and woman in Eden. However, although there is a Heaven to receive souls, there is no such thing as a devil or Hell – instead Reid holds the Spaniards accountable for these notions. Reid argues that the cliché of Indian stoicism springs from their belief that all souls go to a Heaven and that there is no Hell, hence nothing to fear from death. He clears up the strong misconception that local Indians worshipped the eagle and details how they came to revere but not worship it (an example of how Europeans tended to misunderstand Indian customs and values).

LETTER 5 – Food and Personal Appearance

This letter is really an extensive catalogue of food, wild game, fruit and nuts and cultivated crops, even detailing the culinary use of acorns. Reid comments upon body ornament, beads, ear-rings and ear-piercing, and also remarks that the local Indians never pierced the nose. Reid is also a great source of Indian lore, saying here that they never used salt in the belief that it would turn their hair grey, and that they preferred to eat food cold, believing that it preserved their teeth.

LETTER 6 – Marriage

In this letter Reid goes into great detail about polygamy, dowries and the wedding ceremony itself. If a man mistreated his wife, her male relatives could buy her back in order to marry her to someone who would treat her decently. The conversion to Catholicism effectively banished polygamy.

LETTER 7 – Births and Burials

Again important customs are noted. Reid discusses the three-day purification ceremony of mother and newborn infant and comments on the custom that a woman could not share her husband's bed until their child could walk. As in other letters, Reid spares no detail in his burial accounts, including a mention of the whistling noise produced by blowing into the tube of the leg-bone of a deer.

LETTER 8 – Medicine and Diseases

This letter is a fascinating amalgam of diseases, wizardry, cures and potions. Treatments for rheumatism, fevers, inflammation, paralysis, snakebites and many more ailments are listed. Reid observes that syphilis among the Indian people was unknown and that baldness and toothache were very rare. He goes into some detail on the practice of dipping arrows in poison and implies that the medicine men were shrewd psychologists, using deception and placebo when required.

LETTER 9 – Customs

In the long, often painful relationship between Europeans and Indians, the former rarely won enough respect and confidence to witness important tribal rituals and customs; and ignorant observers often attached their own explanations and values to what they were seeing for the first time. Reid's sources, however, were reliable and give him a sense of authority as he recounts his observations of the most sacred of customs.

Hunting was central to native cultures and many rituals surrounded the hunt. Hunters often fasted and were forbidden to eat what they themselves had killed. Physical endurance and resistance to pain were highly respected; conversely physical cowardice in the face of pain was considered

—*From a drawing by Maynard Dixon. Copyright, 1931, Automobile Club of Southern California*

HUGO REID AT THE RANCHO SANTA ANITA

A SCOTCH PAISANO

Hugo Reid's Life in California, 1832–1852 Derived from His Correspondence

SUSANNA BRYANT DAKIN

UNIVERSITY OF CALIFORNIA PRESS

Far Left: Hugo Reid at the Rancho Santa Anita.

Left: A Scotch Paisano: Reid's biography by Susanna Bryant Dakin.

Below: A map encompassing Reid's landholdings in Spanish California.

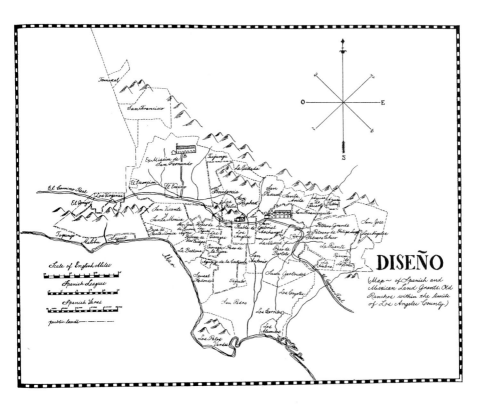

DISEÑO

(Map ~ of Spanish and Mexican Land Grants. Old Ranchos within the limits of Los Angeles County.)

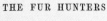

THE FUR HUNTERS

OF THE FAR WEST;

A NARRATIVE OF

ADVENTURES IN THE OREGON AND
ROCKY MOUNTAINS.

BY ALEXANDER ROSS,
AUTHOR OF "ADVENTURES OF THE FIRST SETTLERS ON THE OREGON OR
COLUMBIA RIVER."

IN TWO VOLUMES.

VOL. I.

LONDON:
SMITH, ELDER AND CO., 65, CORNHILL.
1855.

ADVENTURES

OF THE FIRST SETTLERS ON THE

OREGON OR COLUMBIA RIVER:

BEING

A NARRATIVE OF THE EXPEDITION FITTED OUT BY
JOHN JACOB ASTOR,

TO ESTABLISH THE

"PACIFIC FUR COMPANY;"

WITH AN ACCOUNT OF SOME
INDIAN TRIBES ON THE COAST OF THE PACIFIC.

BY ALEXANDER ROSS,
ONE OF THE ADVENTURERS

LONDON:
SMITH, ELDER AND CO., 65, CORNHILL.
1849.

Above: The portrait of Alexander Ross
appearing in his books; examples of two
frontispieces, *left.*

Below: A map showing the routes
and explorations of Ross.

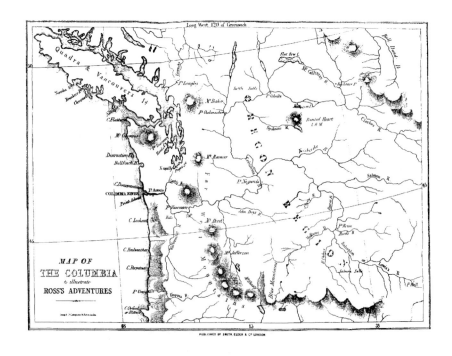

Above: Original etching of Fort Nez Perces from *The Fur Hunters of the Far West* by Ross.

Right: A Nez Perces Indian, portrait by Alfred Jacob Miller (1810–1874).

Left: Alfred Jacob Miller, 'Presents to Indians'

Below: Miller's sketch of an encampment of Shoshone Indians.

Above: Cree Indians, from a watercolour by Peter Rindisbacher (1806-34). (National Archives of Canada/ C-001917)

Right: 'Preparing for a Buffalo Hunt' by Alfred Jacob Miller.

Above: Inside a Cree
Tent, engraved after
a drawing by Robin
Hood. (National
Archives of Canada/
C-001917)

Left: A Crow chief,
drawing taken from
J G Word's *Natural
History*.

Right: 'The Trapper's Bride' by Alfred Jacob Miller.

Below: Miller's view of 'Trappers starting for the Beaver Hunt'.

Above and left: George Catlin's paintings of Mandan Indians, dressed for the Buffalo Dance.

Below, left: Mandan chief, taken from J G Word's *Natural History.*

Above and right: A man's shirt and trousers of quill decorated buckskin, possibly Mandan or from the neighbouring Gros Ventre. (National Museums of Scotland)

disgraceful. Men sometimes lay down on hills of red ants, whose bites were particularly painful, and the ants were often swallowed alive in order to built up resistance to pain.

Reid details verbal feuding whereby families often sang war songs against one another, using 'the most obscene and indecent language imaginable', although the feuding was confined to verbal insults only.

He continues with the observation that local tribes did not travel widely and had little curiosity about far away lands. He also describes the church feast in commemoration of the dead. Possessions were burned in a hole and many others given to those attending. After the deceased's possessions were burned, the hole was covered with earth and the feast ended.

Letter 11 – Barter and Utensils

Reid was a keen observer and able to extract useful details of daily life. Indian money, for example, consisted of seashells strung together, and measurements involved knuckles and wrists. He explains barter systems that rely upon money, fish, sea-otter pelts and utensils; and comments on the manufacture of nets, lines and threads from hemp made from nettles. Other useful materials included bone, shell, cane, granite, soapstone and split rushes.

Letter 12 – Sport and Games

It was well-known that the Native peoples enjoyed athletics and other sports and games, many of which resembled those brought over from Europe, especially games of gambling and guessing. The game *churchchurki* (called *peon* by the Spanish) consisted of trying to guess which hand held a black or white marker. Great wagers were bet on the results of this team game and Reid lists it as the past and present favourite of the tribes. *Chachaukel* was an advanced game of the same type. Other games were variations on dice-throwing. Reid also writes on that sport of special interest to the Scots: 'Football was unknown until after the [Spanish] conquest, when they learned it of the Indians of San Diego.'

LETTER 13 – Tradition

Many traditional tales and legends are similar among the tribal and nomadic peoples of the world, but all but the most astute observers would fail to notice the local or individual influences at play in these tales. This letter tells a delightful story about the deception by six brothers out of seven who had married seven sisters, and what the sisters did to exact their revenge on all but the trustworthy brother.

The sisters turned themselves into stars and became The Pleiades constellation. The lone good brother was allowed to join them, but set apart in Taurus. Although many other cultures relate their own legends of stars and constellations, this particular story is told through the medium of hunting and root-gathering.

It was a common mistake for Europeans to confuse legend and embroidered folk tale with tradition and religious belief.

LETTER 14 – Fable

Two delightful tales are described. The first is 'The Girl enamoured of the Lightning'. Reid called it 'among the most curious' of the traditional tales he was told. A girl is made pregnant by a bolt of lightning and her baby grows into a difficult and argumentative (though wise) man of the tribe. The tribe, however, finally puts him to death.

The second is 'The Coyote and the Water', where a coyote is thoroughly humbled when he discovers he cannot beat a running brook in a race. This tale appears to echo the Greek writer Aesop and his well-known *Fables*.

Reid's contemporary readers may have drawn instant comparisons with folk tales and legends already known to them, and might perhaps have come to recognise that the desires and fears of the Native peoples were not so different from those of Europeans after all.

LETTER 15 – Legend

This is a long letter, recounting a powerful legend about a wizard and his daughter. Reid offers useful comments at the end of the story, and debates which bits of the tale might no longer be believed. Perhaps the modern-day reader may sense, as with Irish or Scottish Gaelic narratives, that the original reciter has orated a tale of great antiquity and is talking about creatures that are no longer understood by Reid's audience. Nonetheless, with little adornment and brief comment, he has clarified details where he believes it necessary, but otherwise lets his readers draw their own conclusions.

LETTER 16 – First Arrival of the Spaniards

This letter marks a turn in Reid's accounts, which previously dealt with the Native peoples alone. It is a remarkable letter in its own right, quickly tracing the disillusionment of the Indians with their Spanish overlords. At first they were impressed by their horses, imagining the riders to be god-like. The women hid, while the men darkened their huts. The Spaniards had flints to make fire, their weapons were powerful, and the Indians named them *Chichinabros*, 'reasonable beings'.

Soon another party of Spanish violated their women, causing the women themselves to feel impure, and the white children born to them were put to death. Conversion to Christianity was the next step, and gifts were offered to the local people to pave the way for religious conversion. Indian courtesy would not permit refusal, but many of the foods given were secretly buried or destroyed.

Reid demonstrates in this letter the dawning realisation by the Indians that these magnificent visitors, with all their marvellous beasts, weapons and foodstuffs, were lacking in many ways. The strange white men were not gods after all, for what god would use firearms to murder small creatures like birds so wantonly? God, the Giver of Life, would surely not need to kill as mere mortals do. 'Reasonable beings' soon gave way to 'having a nasty white colour and having ugly blue eyes'!

LETTER 17 – Conversion

It was natural that the Spanish would carry to the New World the notion of a community surrounding a monastery and being dependent upon it. The mission thus became the centre of life in California and Hugo Reid gives accounts of two in his area, describing the beautiful natural features of the land before and after settlement. Significantly both the river and its enjoining mission were named after the local earthquakes (*temblores*) which were always common, and which were the great fear of Reid's wife. Even the local cattle brand was a 't' for *temblores*.

In this rather blunt letter it is obvious that Reid cannot contain his cynicism as he describes the process of conversion to Catholicism, which he himself had to undertake in order to marry. While the priests considered this a true conversion, Reid says of the Indian people:

> *Poor devils! Not one word of Spanish did they understand – not one word of the Indian tongue did the priest know. They had no more idea that they were worshipping God than an unborn child has of astronomy. Numbers of old men and women have been gathered to the dust of their fathers – and a few still remain – whose whole stock of Spanish was contained in the never-failing address of 'Amar a Dios!' And whose religion, as Catholics, consisted in being able to cross themselves, under an impression it was something connected with hard work and still harder blow. Baptism was called by them* soyna *[sic], 'being bathed', and strange to say, was looked upon, although such a simple ceremony, as being ignominious and degrading.*

Reid was taking a great risk in this account. He was, after all, a public figure in Catholic Los Angeles. But perhaps these were his truest feelings on a matter to which he had only alluded briefly in the past. His wife had suffered greatly at the hands of the local mission and this must have given him a strong motivation for speaking out.

Reid is especially critical about the use of local people, hired as soldiers or servants, to induce more of their tribe to convert. He says that many people were tied up and whipped like cattle, and that children and parents were isolated until they were baptised. He was also puzzled as to why many of the war-like tribes did not resist, but merely hid away. A fine linguist himself he is clearly astonished that the Spanish could not even explain these rites properly, and did not bother to learn any of the native languages;, and of course the Indians themselves did not speak Spanish – so all the conversions were performed in total incomprehension.

Reid does allude to the exception of Padre Jose Maria Zalvidea who, despite his less than gentle approach to the Indians, at least took pains to learn the local language and grammar. He translated prayers, including 'The Lord's Prayer', into the Indian tongue, and even preached in it. Other priests employed translators, but Reid still felt the underlying sympathy was lacking whatever language was used to preach.

LETTER 18 – First Missionary Proceedings

Reid touches on many topics in this letter, like animal husbandry, the planting of crops and vines, irrigation, incoming Indians and their contribution to mission life. He comments that deserters from the mission were flogged and put in chains, and that some runaways preferred to live in the mountains as hunted fugitives rather than return to such cruel treatment. Reid also talks about the building of libraries, but notes rather sadly that his local mission library had been reduced by loss and theft and was 'mere rubbish'.

LETTER 19 – A New Era in Mission Affairs

This letter is a more detailed continuation of the previous one. Reid believed that the arrival of Padre Jose Maria Zalvidea ushered in a more prosperous era. Zalvidea planted gardens and orchards, and improved tree-planting, irrigation and fencing. Husbandry flourished and there were now cattle, sheep and hogs. The Padre seemed to be a capable but harsh ruler over an ever more complex society of shoemakers, blacksmiths, bakers, musicians, brick and tile-makers, weavers, spinners and others. There were also many larger industries including soap-making, tanning and coopering. Reid respected the administrative reforms, but commented pointedly that there was still no doctor.

Reid goes on to list some entertaining notions. He says that Indians used pigs primarily for soap-making because they would not eat the product, claiming that pigs were really just transformed Spaniards. (He adds that the same view prevailed all over Mexico.) Reid also notes that drunkards were flogged only when sober, wizards and shamans were chained and put to work sawing wood, and when couples were heard to quarrel violently they were tied together by the leg until they agreed to get along with one another.

In general Reid did not approve of the cruelty and widespread beating and whipping, and contrasted the Padre's ill-treatment of the Indians with the generous hospitality which was meted out to travellers and guests. Padre Zalvidea, despite his far-sighted progress with local languages, was later transferred elsewhere.

LETTER 20 – Better Times

This letter deals with the succession of Padre Jose Bernardo Sanchez as head of the local mission. Noting the change of attitude towards the local Indians, he comments that better and more humane treatment resulted in less fighting and drunkenness. Rations were freely given and a more general spirit of tolerance prevailed. Reid gives a colourful description of the Highland game of shinty, very popular with the Indians:

After service, on Sunday, football and races were on the carpet until the afternoon, when a game called by the Scotch 'shinty' and I believe by the English 'bandy' took place. One set being composed of all men and one of all women. People flocked in from all parts to see the sport, and heavy bets were made. The priest took a great interest in the game, and as the women seldom had less than half a dozen quarrels, in which hair flew by the handful, it pleased him very much. The game being concluded, all went to prayers, and so ended the Sabbath.

LETTER 21 – Decay of the Mission

By 1834 local missions in general were flourishing, but the Mexican government passed a law secularising them, resulting in land being given away, vineyards destroyed, and a spree of looting of Indian property by Europeans. There was mass desertion by the Indians during these years, brought on by starvation and poverty. Sonorans (a roving population of bandits and opportunists from Sonora, a province in Northern Mexico, who were making life difficult for the Californian authorities in Reid's time) flooded into the area, introducing gambling and drink on a large scale.

LETTER 22 – Finis

The last letter summarises Hugo Reid's aims and purposes in writing the series of letters for the newspaper. He begins:

… having given a sketch of the Angeles County Indians from the time they were free, natal possessors of the soil, living contented in a state of nature, until these civilised times of squatting and legislative oppression, in which not only they but those bearing their blood in a fourth degree are included, to the shame of this our country, and disgrace of the framers of such laws ….

Reid then contrasts pre-Conquest times with his own present in terms of language, religion, morals, food, clothing, social customs and so on. He notes that the Indians always considered Hell a white man's invention, meant exclusively for white people; and they did not see the point of the Resurrection since they believed in a spiritual afterlife for all.

Finally, Reid reminds his readers that this series of letters is not concerned with matters other than those touching upon Indian life.

* * *

Hugo Reid – *A Summary*

Hugo Reid, the businessman, legislator and writer, is still considered to be one of the key pioneers through the major events in California's colourful early history, including war with Mexico, the Gold Rush, and then statehood. Through all this he remained a passionate believer in the rights of his wife's people and spent the last years of his short life researching the customs, language and history of the local Indian tribes. Writing about this topic for his local newspaper, *The Los Angeles Star*, the letters were read avidly by people who took a likeminded view and were determined to see better conditions prevail. Today we may read the letters as fascinating accounts of a vanquished people whose customs and culture were fast disappearing, even in Reid's time. His sources and informants were already very old and very few. Reid himself concluded in his letters:

> *If these sketches of Indian character have been at all interesting to the readers of the* Star, *I shall consider myself amply paid for the time occupied in writing them.*

Susanna Bryant Dakin, in her account of his life, *A Scotch Paisano,* devotes much effort to appraising his achievement:

> *Hugo Reid's informal Indian essays, published as 'Letters to the Los Angeles Star during the year 1852', were widely read and discussed. Several of Reid's friends became sufficiently moved by his depiction of the Indians' sad plight to contribute toward the printing, in the same year, of Don Benito Wilson's humane and constructive report as United States Indian agent in the Southwest.*

She continues:

Obviously, Hugo Reid's letters about his wife's people reached much farther and deeper than he ever dreamed they would. Even within the few months of life that were left to him, after their publication, he saw gratifying evidence of interest in the Indians, aroused by his own pen.

Dakin details many such ripples, including a long essay by one Philo on the plight of the Indians, which owes its origin to Reid's letters. Other famous men who appreciated Reid's accomplishments included John Nugent, writer and editor of *The San Francisco Herald*, who said:

Of a good education, a fine mind, and a most remarkable memory, Hugo Reid possessed a fund of information concerning the history of California surpassing that of almost any other man in the state. No man certainly had an equal acquaintance with the history of the Indians.

Even today's reader must be impressed by the bold and confident tone of Reid's letters. It must have taken a lot of courage to criticise ecclesiastical and civil authorities of the day; and to publicise his conviction that Indian people were a sophisticated race who deserved more respect for their beliefs and customs than they received. The true 'savages', in Reid's eyes, were those who exploited the knowledge and goodwill of the native people.

Reid belonged to a level of society where he could easily have ignored the treatment of the local people. However, he had experienced prejudice at first hand. Married to a native woman, he found himself defending their land and property at all times from a political climate that dictated no indigenous person should have property rights, or indeed any other rights afforded to European society.

It is unfortunate that his true calling as a journalist and writer eluded him until the last year of his life. His achievement is no less for that. His view that all men are equal under the skin is a notion long held by Scotland's favourite poets and writers. Reid's ultimate contribution was probably an extension of beliefs formed in Scotland, sharpened and expanded during his years in South America and Mexico. As Robert Burns wrote, 'a man's a man for all that'.

Chapter 4
Alexander Ross

THE life of Alexander Ross was intimately tied up with the successes and failures of the American and Canadian fur industries. Ross was involved with all three of the leading companies of his day, and served each with loyalty and distinction. Yet unlike many of his contemporaries in the fur trade, he did not emigrate with that particular trade in mind.

Ross was born on his father's farm in Morayshire, Layhill, in the parish of Dyke on 9 May 1783. He left Scotland on the ship *Countess of Darlington* in 1804, sailing out of Greenock to arrive in Quebec in July. There he worked as a schoolmaster and later found the same employment in Glengarry, Upper Canada.

In 1809 Ross bought 300 acres of land with the intention of farming as his father before him in Scotland. However it was the up-and-coming fur trade that seemed to offer more promise of wealth in the New World. So Ross signed up as a clerk with a man called Wilson Price Hunt of the newly-founded Pacific Fur Company, a subsidiary of John Jacob Astor's American Fur.

Ross sailed from Montreal to New York with other employees of Pacific Fur, before departing on the *Tonquin* on 6 September 1810 bound for the Pacific Coast and the site of Astor's proposed fur post on the mouth of the Columbia River. The ship almost did not arrive. In addition to rough seas and near shipwreck, the *Tonquin*'s captain, John Thorn, was an abrasive fellow who was not above putting the safety of his passengers at risk. When the ship put into the Falklands for fresh water, Thorn deliberately left Ross and eight others behind and they were forced to pursue the ship through very rough seas. Ross commented later that he owed his life to Robert Stuart, another Scot on board the *Tonquin*, who forced Thorn at gunpoint to turn back and pick up the men following in their wake. The *Tonquin* finally arrived in late March of 1811, and Ross began his work, helping to establish Fort Astoria beside the Columbia River.

Shortsighted mismanagement after the War between Britain and America made trade difficult for Astor and he was forced to sell Fort Astoria and another fort, Okanagan, to the North West Company in 1813. Having proved his worth Ross was put in charge of the newly-acquired Fort Okanagan. It was there that Ross married a local Okanagan Indian woman, popularly known as Sally, to whom he remained devoted throughout his life. (Later records show that they were married again on 24 December 1828, this time by Christian rite, and that they raised a family of at least 13 children. Their son, William, became a very influential civic figure in the Canadian west, as did son James and daughters Mary and Jemima).

In 1818, after earlier exploration by others of the lucrative Snake Indian country, Ross was involved in the founding and running of a new fort, Nez Perces, at the gateway to the area, on the site of present-day Walla Walla, Washington State. When the North West merged with Hudson's Bay in 1821, Ross continued at Nez Perces with the new company until 1823 when he took part in an expedition into the interior of Snake country, in what is now mainly Idaho, right to the mouth of the Boise River. In 1824 he embarked on a second expedition, this time as leader. The expedition features heavily in his writings, and the account of his experiences was to become an invaluable source book for traders, settlers and scouts.

In 1825 Sir George Simpson of the Hudson's Bay Company decided that Ross was not the man to develop further the Snake River country and he was effectively 'retired'. Ross was offered a land grant in the Red River Colony near present-day Winnipeg, Manitoba in Canada.

Still loosely affiliated to Hudson's Bay, but now free to look for alternative means to earn a living, Ross took part in hunting expeditions to supplement the diet of the white settlers. He soon began to trade, an activity that he continued for the rest of the decade.

Ross later became a sheriff before being appointed commander of the volunteer army to help maintain order in the Red River Colony. Later, as a councillor, he acted as a moderating influence on the many disputes involving free traders and trading monopolies in the area, as well as any religious conflicts that arose. Ross, however, became too embroiled in trade issues and was forced to resign as sheriff and councillor.

Throughout, Ross remained a popular figure, particularly with the Metis (mixed European and Native population), and in this capacity he probably helped to avert serious political trouble.

Ross was no doubt under great pressure to trade ruthlessly in order to make money for very tough employers. But he also had more than a grudging admiration for the people he found himself having to out-wit and out-fight to further his career in the fur trade. The time that he devoted to learning and observing native customs must have sometimes made his employers impatient for quicker dividends, but Ross appeared to understand how a hasty approach often backfires, and he continued to point the way forward, urging patience and forbearance.

However, he was also a man of his times, and the use of words such as 'barbarism', 'heathen' and 'savage' to describe the local peoples in his writings does present some difficulties for the modern reader. Like many of his contemporaries, Ross believed that it was his duty to bring civilisation, enlightenment and Victorian values to the peoples he encountered. He was a son of the Empire and often wrote like one, with an endless stiff-upper-lip and 'white man's burden' approach. Yet for all this Ross managed to overcome many of his own social prejudices, and repeatedly we can detect genuine sympathy for the customs and cultures around him. Ross's marriage to an Indian woman, his life-long devotion to her, and his obvious admiration for her people, are evident throughout his work.

Ross died at Red River on 23 October 1856, leaving his writings as an enduring legacy of his times. His entry in *Appleton's Cyclopaedia of American Biography* concludes thus:

> *Ross was a man of exceptional abilities and was greatly esteemed by all who knew him, white and red alike. For the first fourteen years of the white man's occupation of Oregon, he was an energetic and influential participant in the activities of the region, and for the history of a considerable part of the period he remains almost the sole first-hand authority.*

* * *

Alexander Ross – *The Writings*

Adventures of the First Settlers

In 1849 Alexander Ross published *Adventures of the First Settlers on the Oregon or Columbia River: being a narrative of the expedition fitted out by John Jacob Astor to Establish the 'Pacific Fur Company'; with an account of some Indian Tribes on the coast of the Pacific, by Alexander Ross, one of the adventurers.* His preface explains much about his subsequent style:

> *In presenting the present work to the public, I have no very sanguine expectations. All I am attempting is to lay before my readers a faithful and impartial statement of what took place, during my own times, in a quarter hitherto but little known.*

In the early chapters Ross sets the background to Astor's founding of the Pacific Fur Company and its base at Fort Astoria. He tells how he, at 28 years old, set sail from New York on the *Tonquin* in 1810, bound for the proposed site of the Fort at the mouth of the Columbia River. The voyage was dangerous, with rough seas, near shipwreck and mutiny, but the *Tonquin* finally reached its destination, the Oregon coastline, in late March 1811. Ross was now ready to begin the real challenge of exploring new territory for the fur industry.

By chapter five Ross begins to describe the customs of the people of the Columbia River region. He lists the ten key tribes of the area and goes into great detail about their laws, dress, games and treatment of slaves. He covers topics as diverse as superstitions, sturgeon-fishing and the making of baskets. Ross also adds details about the Chinook, Clatsop and Cathlamux peoples, noting their economic dependence on salmon-fishing. Of the Chinook, for example, he writes (*Adventures of the First Settlers* [*AFS*], page 87):

> *The Chinooks are crafty and intriguing …. Nor are they less ingenious than inquisitive; the art they display in the making of canoes, of* pagods [wooden deities], *and of fishing tackle, and other instruments, deserves commendation. They show much skill in carved work.*

> *The men are generally stout, muscular and strong … their dress invariably consists of a loose garment, made of the skin of the woodrat …. All classes wear the* cheapool, *or hat, which is made of a tough strong kind of grass and is waterproof.*

The females are excessively fond of singing and adorning their persons with fantastic trinkets. All classes marry very young ... children are suckled at the breast until their second or third year ... the women have also their own amusements. Their chief game, called 'omintook' is played by two only, with four beaver teeth, curiously marked and numbered on one side, which they throw like dice.

On the matter of Chinook money, he adds:

The circulating medium in use among them is a small white shell called higua, *about two inches long, of a convex form ... it is thin, light and durable ... so high are the* higua *prized that I have seen six of two-and-a-half inches long refused for a new gun. But of late since the whites came among them, the beaver skin called* enna, *has been added to the currency; so that by these two articles, which form the medium of trade, all property is valued.*

He explains the custom of flattening the heads of babies, for reasons of beauty, by the gradual application of splints during infancy. Many northwest tribes followed this custom, although it is interesting that the so-called 'Flathead' Indians did not follow this practice. Their name is derived from the distinctive signage used to denote the tribe: the placement of the hands flat against the head.

Ross, like many of his Scottish colleagues in the fur industry, had a genuine interest in the languages of the peoples he encountered, which transcended any practical dealings. He noted in his book that 'the language spoken by these people is guttural, very difficult for a foreigner to learn and equally hard to pronounce. To speak the Chinook dialect, you must be a Chinook'. With some modesty perhaps, he refuses to comment on his own success with the language, although his linguistic ability was known to have averted trouble on several occasions during future expeditions and encounters.

Ross also establishes himself in his writing as a man with an insatiable curiosity, though it is fair to say that his anecdotal style is rather stilted. In striving after historical truth, it often lacks excitement. Here he writes on matters as diverse as rattlesnakes and tobacco:

The ground here is everywhere full, covered with flat stones, and wherever these stones lie, and indeed elsewhere, the rattlesnakes are very numerous. At times they may be heard hissing all around so that we had to keep a sharp look-out to avoid treading on them; but the natives appeared to have no dread of them. As soon as one appears, the Indians fix its head to the ground with a small forked stick round the neck, then extracting the fang or poisonous part, they take the reptile into their bosoms, play with it and let it go again. Here we staid [sic] for the night on some rocks infested with innumerable rattlesnakes, which caused us not a little uneasiness during the night.

As he chronicles the failure of the Pacific Fur's Fort Astoria, Ross introduces some great characters onto his human stage, including a man known as Donald 'Perpetual Motion' Mackenzie, one of his heroes. Born in Cromarty in 1783, Mackenzie entered the service of the North West Company before working with Astor. Charismatic and much loved by the people he traded with, he spoke many languages and was a remarkable hunter and tracker. Despite weighing 25 stones he was reputed to be fit and agile, surviving drowning, starvation, attack by Indians, and a life of nearly continuous privation. Ross describes him thus:

To trade a day's journey on snow shoes was his delight but [he] detested spending five minutes scribbling in a journal. His travelling notes were often kept on a beaver skin written hieroglyphically with a pencil or piece of coal. When not asleep he was always upon foot strolling backwards and forwards ... so peculiar was his pedestrian habit that he was known by the name of Perpetual Motion. (AFS, page 283)

Ross marvels at Mackenzie's retrieval of a stolen rifle against all odds, by marching straight into an Indian camp, regardless of the dangers.

His open, free and easy manner often disarmed the most daring savages. He would stroll among them unarmed and alone.' (AFS, page 130)

Mackenzie died in Maysville, New York in 1851 and was immortalised in Washington Irving's book, *Astoria*:

[Mackenzie] had a frame seasoned to toils and hardship, a spirit not to be intimidated, and was reputed to be a remarkable shot, all of which gave him renown on the frontier.

Ross also gives an account of the Okanagan Indians, his wife's people. He describes their spiritual beliefs and ceremonies:

The religion of the Oakinackens [Ross's own spelling], *like that of all Indian tribes, is difficult to understand, and still more difficult to explain. They however believe in a good and evil spirit, who presides over the destinies of man, and that all good actions are rewarded and all evil deeds punished in future state.* (*AFS*, page 286ff)

They have no places of worship, public or private. They believe that this world will have an end ... the land will float again, like the island of their forefathers, and then all must perish – the 'its-owl-eigh', *or 'end of the world'.*

He comments on Indian uses for wild hemp, and in the next chapters covers topics as diverse as family life, feuding, medicines and herbs, types of gambling, marriage and burial customs, mourning, and details of food like fish, roots and berries.

The men lead an active life; between hunting, fishing, war and making canoes ... nor are the women less busy – curing fish, drying meat, dressing leather, collecting roots and firewood ... each family is ruled by the joint authority of the husband and wife, but more particularly by the latter. At their meals they generally eat separately, men, women and children in that order. (*AFS*, page 295)

The Oakinacken are by no means ferocious or cruel, either in looks, habits or dispositions, but are, on the contrary, rather an easy, mild and agreeable people. (*AFS*, page 292)

Their implements of warfare are guns, bows and arrows (in the use of which they are very expert) shields, knives, and lances, and a bludgeon, for close combat, called a spampt. (*AFS*, page 318)

... Gambling, dancing, horse-racing and frolicking, in all its varied forms, continued without intermission. (*AFS*, page 315)

A common mode of counting with them is by snows or winters ... each finger stands for ten years. (*AFS*, page 324)

Ross's accounts touch upon Indian name-changing and time-keeping. He stresses, using the former as an example, that most customs that appear strange to Europeans were quite logical to Native peoples. The changing of names may appear odd, for example, but it actually chronicles an individual's progress through life, from being fast and agile as a youngster to old and wise as an elder. Similarly, it charts a person's standing within the tribe and how his peers view him or her throughout life. Conventionally, however, Ross seems to check his narrative and attribute this custom to mere whim, commenting: 'Indians of all classes change their names periodically, taking new ones according to fancy or caprice.' (*AFS*, page 324)

The final chapters reveal much about Ross's true attitudes. Whatever his official position on manifest destiny and the role of civilisation, Ross's respect for Indian laws and customs is undeniable: 'Reason and right, humanity and forbearance are as often to be found among the savages themselves as among the whites.' (*AFS*, page 328) He continues: 'There are many traits of virtue to be found in the Indian character. They are brave, generous and often charitable.' Then, almost scandalously for his time, he notes for his readers (page 322):

> *There is less crime in an Indian camp of 500 souls than there is in a civilised village of but half that number … theft in particular is held in the utmost abhorrence, so that it rarely occurs among them.*

The word 'civilised', when taken in the context of the author's upbringing, appears to be used ironically, making this an extraordinary statement that must have shocked any Victorian reader looking to reinforce his or her own prejudices and attitude of superiority.

The concluding chapters about his time with Pacific Fur probably reveal Ross struggling with his own prejudices. This is illustrated by his concern that Indian children required a European education, even though it was not particularly appropriate for their future needs. He cites the instance of two Flathead children whom he personally took to the Red River Colony to be educated.

Ross is clearly intrigued by these people who have survived so well for so long in an environment that can be fickle and deadly. He exhibits a genuine desire to understand and explain his observations as well as he can, perhaps a trait of the inquisitive schoolteacher.

The sale of Fort Astoria to the North West Company marked the end of this particular narrative and set the stage for Ross's next work.

The Fur Hunters of the Far West – VOLUME 1

The second book by Alexander Ross, *The Fur Hunters of the Far West: a narrative of adventures in the Oregon and Rocky Mountains in two volumes* (*FHFW*), published in London in 1855, takes up Ross's story at the end of his employment with Astor's Pacific Fur, the decline of Fort Astoria, and the beginning of his involvement with the North West Company.

In his preface (dedicated to Sir George Simpson as Governor of the merged company), Ross resumes the language he used previously, using words and phrases like 'savage', 'primeval barbarism', and so on. However it soon becomes clear that while Ross is trying to relate to his audience on one hand, he is also making a genuine attempt to portray what he has actually observed and learned:

> ... *the Author of the following sheets has spent the last 44 years of his life without a single day's intercession in the Interior territories of North America .... Under so many successive changes, the aboriginal tribes, once so formidable, are fast melting away. Soon all traces of the past will be in the memorials which the pen has preserved, what he has written is fact and not fiction: real wild life not romance.*

Thus setting the tone, Ross begins the account of his work for the North West Company, covering topics as diverse as wolves, women on horseback, hostilities between rival fur companies, feasting, bear grease, and the taste of dog's flesh.

His account of wolves is every bit as politically incorrect to the modern-day reader as some of his comments on the tribes. His wolves are slavering, fanged creatures that have more in common with Little Red Riding Hood than the canny, shy animals who are particularly wary of human beings. To the Indian people, wolves are often portrayed as guardian spirits

Writing about the wives of two French trappers plotting an escape from Indians on horseback, Ross notes that 'women in these parts are as expert as men on horseback' (*FHFW*, page 22); and in chapter three he goes on to give a classic description of an Indian banquet with dogs 'yawning, howling and growling', and where 'only one knife is used' to cut meat and to eat with.

However, most of the time Ross is concerned with the North West Pacific tribes in so far as they helped or hindered the fur trade, and how diplomatic relations between the traders and the tribes had to be based on mutual respect and a working knowledge of local language and culture.

Here, for example, is the proper protocol for dealing with local chieftains:

> *You untie his shoes and dry his socks. You next hand him good water and tobacco; and you must smoke along with him. After which you must listen with grave attention to all he has got to say. Nor must you forget that Indians are acute observers of men and things.* (*FHFW*, page 169)

Continuing with his stories of adventure, Donald Mackenzie appears once again. According to Ross, both men were considered crack shots: 'We killed seven bears, nine wolves and eleven small deer,' Ross comments with some pride.

Chapter six of *The Fur Hunters of the Far West* describes Ross's second expedition into the Snake Country and his work at Fort Nez Perces, when he was left in charge. He describes the building of the fort in character-istic detail, and gives a compelling account of the nuts-and-bolts of fur trapping as a business.

Chapter eight is also of special interest, and shows Ross at his best as an amateur ethnologist, stating that the Snake peoples 'are complete masters of what is called the cabalistical language of birds and beasts and can imitate to the utmost perfection the singing of birds and the howling of wolves' (*FHFW*, pages 250-51). Ross further notes that 'the Snakes prefer their own tobacco to ours', and that he learned very quickly about the significance of tobacco amongst the western tribes, in rites and cere-monies, and as a thread of communication between the real world and spirit world. Tobacco is noted as a gift or enticement or offering of appeasement to spirits or men. It always indicated reverence and under-standing, and fur trappers quickly became aware of its protocol among the tribes. Since generally men and women were allowed to smoke, but children were not, tobacco became a rite of passage for young members of the tribes approaching adulthood.

The book then takes the reader through the 1821 merger of the North West with Hudson's Bay, before ending the first volume with various accounts of local tribes, reflecting on the beauty of some Indian women and the problems experienced by half-breed or *brule* children – orphans of fur trappers and local women. These children were often rejected by both communities and Ross was concerned about their future education, reli-gious upbringing, and ultimately their choice of community. This was a subject close to his heart as his own children were the product of a mixed marriage and he had worked hard to ensure they enjoyed the full benefit of education and training.

Ross also observes the head-dresses, weapons and horses of the local tribes and devotes space to describing the taking and treatment of slaves. However his strongest contribution to an understanding of native culture appears in the 'Vocabulary of the Languages Spoken by the Nez Perces and the Tribes Inhabiting the Country about the Great Forks of the Columbia River', which appears in the Appendix to the first volume.

The Fur Hunters of the Far West – VOLUME 2

Ross's first expedition into the Snake River country, under the auspices of the merged Hudson's Bay Company, had been as part of a party led by one Finan McDonald in 1823. McDonald had relied heavily on the intelligence and stamina of the extraordinary aforementioned Donald 'Perpetual Motion' Mackenzie. A second expedition, this time led by Ross, and without Mackenzie who had left the company, departed from Flathead Post in what is now the state of Montana on 10 February 1824. The date of departure was based on the supposition that hostile Indians would be less active in the heart of a Rocky Mountain winter.

Volume 2 recounts that journey into the country defined by the Snake River and its tributaries. The Snake flows through spectacular mountain country until it meets the Columbia and forms the boundary between much of the modern states of Oregon and Washington, until it finally reaches the sea.

Ross frequently downplays the hazards encountered by his party. As an author who has lived in this region I can only imagine what it might have been like at the time of the Ross expedition. Even today, winter temperatures can plummet to minus 50 degrees fahrenheit. There are still grizzly bears and cougars, and many of the wilderness areas remain unexplored. A hermit was discovered on the Salmon River in the 1960s. It appeared that he had been living undisturbed in his own settlement since the Depression in the 1920s. Giant sturgeon weighing several hundred pounds are still caught in the Snake River, and its cliffs harbour abundant rattlesnake lairs. It would be difficult for even modern explorers to survive these regions in bad weather. On their epic journey a few decades earlier in 1804-06, Lewis and Clarks' expedition travelled through the Snake River country. Even then it was not considered ludicrous that President Thomas Jefferson, a remarkable intellectual who had commissioned the expedition, harboured notions about Lewis and Clark stumbling upon mammoths or mastodons or other prehistoric wonders.

Ross's curiously low-key narrative style now takes us through a spree of killings, scalping and 'horrid cruelties' including snowstorms, blizzards, marauding wild animals, and the practical difficulties of leading a party, including 25 women and 64 children, with 212 beaver traps and 392 horses, through a wild western landscape that had never been explored before. The expedition covered 3450 miles in total.

Volume 2 of *The Fur Hunters of the Far West* was published 31 years after the 1824 Snake River expedition which it describes. During my research I was fortunate enough to obtain a copy of a journal in possession of the Hudson's Bay headquarters in Lime Street, London, that had been printed in the 'Quarterly of the Oregon Historical Society', volume 14, December 1913. This journal provides a useful *précis* of the longer published account of the expedition and is worth looking at in some detail. To set the scene, the first entry is for 10 February and it lists the original party. Ross is the only Scotsman; all the rest are French Canadian. Ross begins:

> *Snow 18 inches deep. Weather cold. Many of these people are too old for a long voyage and very indifferent trappers …. Deep snows and bad weather also made for bad morale ….*

> *Tuesday 17th. Left camp early, the people grumbling to remain. Passed three lodges of Tete Pletes. Francois Rivet caught a beaver; but the wolves devoured it, skin and all ….*

> *Saturday 21st. Antoine Valle's boy died ….*

Ross demonstrates his acute powers of observation:

> *Thursday 11th March. Proceeding over slippery stone road, at every bend a romantic scene opens. The river alone prevents the hills embracing …. Here a curiosity called the Ram's Horn … out of a large pine five feet from root projects a ram's head, the horns of which are transfixed to the middle. The natives cannot tell when this took place but tradition says when the first hunter passed this way, he shot an arrow at a mountain ram and wounded*

him; the animal turned on his assailant who jumped behind a tree. The animal missing, its aim pierced the tree with his horns and killed himself. The horns are crooked and very large. The tree appears to have grown round the horns. Proceeded over zigzag road ....

Saturday 20th. In the evening the cry of 'enemies, enemies, Blackfeet! Piegans' was vociferated in the camp. All hands rushed out when the enemies proved to be six friendly Nez Perces separated from their camp on the buffalo ground and in snow shoes made way to us across the mountains. They have been five days on this journey. They told us the Blackfeet and Piegans had stolen horses out of the Flathead and Nez Perces' camp nine different times and they were preaching up peace and good fellowship. The Blackfeet had made a war excursion against the Snakes, killed eight, taken some slaves and many horses.

Saturday, 19 June, 1825. I invited them [Piegans] to a smoke. They said the camp was not far off and the party 100 strong ... after dark they entertained us to music and dancing all of which we could have dispensed with. Our people threw away thirty-two beaver; twenty were brought in. A strong guard for the horses. All slept armed.

Sunday 20th. Again invited the Piegans to smoke; gave them presents; and told them to set off and play no tricks for we would follow them to their own land to punish them. They saddled horses and sneaked off one by one along the bushes for 400 yards then took to the mountains ....

August 24th. Number of miles traversed to date, 1050; number of horses lost, 18 ....

Tuesday, 12th Oct. This morning after an illness of twenty days during which we carried him on a stretcher died Jean Bat Boucher, aged 65, an honest man.

Ross arrived back at Flathead Post in Montana on Friday, 26 November 1824. His diary entry for 29 November 1824 provides an interesting census of the Flathead Post.

Indians are now as follows there:
Flatheads, 42 lodges, men and lads 168, guns 180, women 70, children 68.
Pend Orielles, lodges 34, men and lads 108, guns 40, women 68, children 71.
Kouttannais, lodges 36, men and lads 114, guns 62, women 50, children 48.
Nez Perces, lodges 12, men and lads 28, guns 20, women 15, children 23.
Spokanes lodges 4, men and lads 12, guns 6, women 7, children 11 and 1850 horses.

Tuesday 30. About 10 o'clock the Flatheads in a body mounted, arrived, chanting the song of peace. At a little distance they halted and saluted the fort with discharges from their guns. We returned the compliment with our brass pounder. The reverberating sound had a fine effect. The head chief advanced and made a fine speech welcoming the white man to these lands, apologising for having but few beaver. The cavalcade then moved up. The chiefs were invited to the house to smoke. All the women arrived on horseback loaded with provisions and a brisk trade began which lasted till dark. The result was, 324 beaver, 154 bales of meat, 159 buffalo tongues, etc.

On Christmas day he noted that there were, 'Considerable Indians. The peace pipe kept in motion. All the people a dram.'

On Hogmanay he observed, 'At daybreak the men saluted with guns. They were treated to rum and cake, each a pint of rum and a half pound of tobacco.'

On Saturday, 12 March 1825, Ross began the eastward journey that would take him to his 100 acres land grant at Red River, effectively ending his role as an officer in the fur trade. He writes:

After breakfast embarked 4 canoes in sight of 1000 natives for Spokane House. 1644 large beaver, 378 small beaver, 29 otter, 775 muskrats, 9 foxes, 1 martin, 8 mink, also leather and provisions.

Ross touches upon on his removal from command by Sir George Simpson, who thought him incapable of making business profitable in the country he had so ably explored. Ross was replaced by Peter Skene Ogden who would lead all further expeditions into Snake country.

This journal shows that Ross appeared capable of applying the same moral code to all men. Dishonesty and duplicity he condemns in his own people as well as Indians. To him, as to most trappers, Native peoples were simply friends or enemies according to their individual loyalties.

Thus his books are perhaps not so much the observations of an enlightened liberal or tolerant sociologist, but a faithful, and fascinating, record of a past that is gone forever.

Later in the book Ross provides a defence for the less influential Snake Indians against their critics, arguing that their tribe had suffered from persecution by Blackfeet and other warlike Indians. He devotes some time at this point to a discussion of the Snake language.

The book then moves its focus to Canada and Ross's ultimate destination of Fort Garry on the site of the Red River Colony. He freely admits his disappointment with the setting and physical appearance of the fort, noting 'nothing but a few wooden houses huddled together without regard for taste or even comfort'.

The Red River Colony

Ross's arrival at Fort Garry brings us to his final volume: *The Red River Settlement: Its Rise, Progress and Present State*. This volume, published in 1849, is a straightforward account of the events that lead up to the establishment of the settlement near the site of present-day Winnipeg, with some additional accounts of local Indians such as the Saulteaux and Cree. It is an important local history, offering some rare insights into the development of the settlement into a thriving community. His comments on the Indians, on the other hand, are rather cursory and incidental to the narrative. Ross's reputation as an amateur ethnologist rests with his first two volumes rather than this final book.

* * *

ALEXANDER ROSS – *A Summary*

Alexander Ross does not fit a preconceived image of a progressive and modern liberal, politically correct in every way. He was the product of a time when aboriginal peoples were considered either obstacles to progress or the subject of pity or ridicule. His use of language illustrates how far he was from modern notions of equality; yet Ross's defence of native customs and laws, as well as the integrity of his descriptions and accounts, argue in his favour. He did not embellish or enhance; and he paid a great deal of attention to facts and detail, providing a valuable legacy for modern readers.

Though touching on most topics, like religion, medicine and commerce, Ross's main interest was language. This was for practical reasons. He was not a linguist, nor even altruistic; he was simply aware that a working knowledge of Indian languages was good for a trapper's business. It is interesting, however, that he continued to publish his lists of vocabulary long after the fur trade was considered viable in the west.

Ross also served to remind his Victorian audiences that missionary practices were on the whole ineffective and moreover prejudicial to everyone concerned; and that Indian peoples often had intricate codes and laws that were more humane than those of so-called 'civilisation'.

The work of Alexander Ross still stands up to scrutiny after all this time. When we read about his devotion to his Okanagan Indian wife; or conjure up an image of him smoking an Indian pipe, or drying a chief's socks, or eating wolf or dog meat, we can almost detect that Ross is desperate to be bolder and more imaginative, but is ultimately bound by the conventions of his day. However, his respect for the Native peoples he worked with, at peace or at war, is never far from the surface.

Chapter 5
Charles McKenzie

HUGO Reid and Alexander Ross had much in common including their interest in the peoples they lived among and their marriages to Indian women. Charles McKenzie is further proof that the Scottish attitude about Native peoples was derived from a true mosaic of individual experiences.

Of the three McKenzie's viewpoint probably appeals most to the modern reader. His writings also show the most flair and individuality. He was an eccentric and unselfconscious man, neither aspiring to respectability like Reid, nor paying too much homage to prevailing philosophies of Victorian society like Ross. However, his attitude had not always been so liberal and it took an experience of prejudice against his own way of life to effect that change.

Born in Ferintosh, Easter Ross in *c*.1778, Charles McKenzie was one of many young Highlanders who experienced the drastic changes to his homeland in the aftermath of the Battle of Culloden (1746) and then the Clearances which were in full swing while McKenzie was still in Scotland. Some of those affected by the evictions and the harsh social climate of the times, found themselves leaving their homeland bound for America and Canada, and many of the fur-trapping dynasties sprang from places like Easter Ross. Names such as Mackenzie/McKenzie, Farquharson, Finlayson, McTavish and Simpson were not uncommon in the business.

It is likely that McKenzie was attracted to the fur trade by stories he heard from relatives, friends, neighbours and kinsmen affected by the emigration of family members. It is known that McKenzie had a distant relative, Roderick MacKenzie, who may have had some influence on Charles' decision to enlist in the fur trade in Canada, but more probably McKenzie was simply following a career opportunity that was open to many young Highlanders at a time when employment seemed a bleak prospect in their own land. Although contracts and terms of service for employment abroad would often be negotiated in Scotland before leaving, it is recorded that McKenzie was engaged as an apprentice clerk by McTavish, Frobisher and Company, a subsidiary firm of the North West Company, and he signed his contract on 30 December 1802 in Montreal.

In October 1804 McKenzie went west to the Red and Assiniboine rivers, and later that year he was sent on an expedition to the Upper Missouri to trade with the Mandans and Gros Ventre Indians, about whom he was to write a great deal. While wintering with the tribes he met with members of the Lewis and Clark expedition (see page 60). Then, in 1805, having successfully completed the first of four expeditions to the Missouri River, he returned to Fort Assiniboine.

Even this early in his career with North West, McKenzie displayed attitudes that would be held against him all his working life. He openly admired and adopted the Indian way of life, and as a result was chastised and viewed with suspicion by his superiors in the fur trade. Undeterred McKenzie stuck to his guns: 'Let any man living with the Indians take the idea of Savage from his mind and he will find their dress much more convenient.'

This period of McKenzie's life inspired journals that detailed his vast knowledge of the native peoples of North America. Like Alexander Ross, McKenzie worked among many different tribes and his observations of Indian life on the Upper Missouri provided especially useful insights of expeditions to the far west.

When the North West Company grew dissatisfied with low profits in the Missouri area, McKenzie was transferred from Fort Assiniboine to take over command of the Lac Seul post in Upper Canada, near Lake Nipigon. It was clear from the outset that this post, considered mainly a crossroads or convenient stopover, would never be as lucrative or productive as others in the area; and McKenzie noted many instances of younger, less experienced men being promoted ahead of him in the Company.

A more sinister motivation for his transfer may have been racial. McKenzie had taken a wife, Mary McKay, the daughter of Scots trader William McKay and a Metis Indian woman called Josette Latour. McKenzie and Mary married 'according to the custom of the country', sometime before 1805. She bore him four children – a son, Hector Aeneas, and three daughters, Julia, Margaret and Catherine – and the marriage lasted for 50 years.

It was common for some traders and trappers to treat such marriage arrangements as mere convenience and to annul them if circumstances dictated. Traders returning to Scotland often left their native wives and children behind. When North West merged with Hudson's Bay, a new rule was drawn up, stating that the new company would no longer maintain native wives and children of their employees. (Although daughter of a mixed marriage, Mary was classified as 'native' rather than 'half-breed' in company records.) This rule outraged McKenzie and he resigned in 1823.

As a result, he and Mary were forced to have two of their daughters, Julia and Margaret, adopted by an aunt and uncle who could offer them the opportunity of an education. They never saw the girls again. Such bitter first-hand experience of prejudice was bound to influence McKenzie's writings on the native peoples.

After his resignation McKenzie lived in Montreal where he formally married Mary McKay in March 1824. In 1844 he returned to his position at the Lac Seul trading post, still a relatively unproductive site; and unprecedented in the Hudson's Bay company annals, Mary McKenzie was left in charge of the trading post for an entire summer, looking after the financial accounts.

Both McKenzie and Mary, it is recorded, helped to combat a series of small-pox epidemics in the settlement. McKenzie caught the illness but survived, while his wife courageously nursed the sick and dying at Lac Seul which had been converted into a hospital.

Having retired to the Red River Colony in 1854, McKenzie died in 1855 and was buried there. His wife survived him by over two decades.

* * *

Charles McKenzie – *The Writings*

McKenzie is the most difficult of the three men to research. His journals are kept in various archives and have been published only in part. His writings are not as substantial as the works of Alexander Ross; nor did his journals achieve the popularity afforded the newspaper accounts of Hugo Reid. However, McKenzie's writings are extremely appealing because of their flair and individuality.

The journal accounts were not published until 1889-90, nearly 50 years after they were forwarded to his kinsman, Roderick MacKenzie, in 1842. McKenzie wrote to Roderick at the time: 'I am sensible that their greatest merit consists in their veracity.'

McKenzie, like Reid and Ross, went to North America as a young man and never returned to Scotland. His journals, written while living among the Indians of the Upper Missouri, convey the impressions of a youthful Scot untainted with preconceptions about what to expect.

His account of the first of his four expeditions describes his experience of joining a small exploratory party to assess the possibilities of trade. Unwittingly he records details of historical significance when he meets the members of the Lewis and Clark expedition. Some knowledge of that expedition is useful when reading McKenzie's work, as it had a profound impact on Native Americans, and on subsequent relations between Europeans and Indians. Lewis and Clark and their party were among the first white men to be witnessed by many tribes and lasting impressions were created. These impressions, however, were not always favourable.

Probably the best example is that of John Colter. Colter went west with Lewis and Clark in 1804. Unlike other members of the expedition, Colter did not return to the eastern settlements at the end of the journey, but remained in the west as a trapper and explorer. Many consider him to be the first so-called 'mountain man', and his exploits are still heralded today. However Colter did not have the mountains all to himself and he became embroiled in a fierce gun battle between the Crow and the Blackfeet tribes, who were traditional mountain enemies. When Colter's presence among the Crow was noted by the retreating Blackfeet, he was wounded. Abandoned to his fate by the erstwhile friendly Crow, Colter had to hobble alone for 300 miles through dangerous country.

The Blackfeet, however, never forgot the sight of the strange white man fighting with their arch enemies and exacted revenge accordingly, accounting for later conflict in relations between Scots and Native peoples.

The Lewis and Clark Expedition

At the time McKenzie could not have known the significance of the Lewis and Clark expedition. On Easter Monday 1803 one of the greatest land sales in history took place when France sold the whole of the Louisiana

Territory to the American president Thomas Jefferson. This new land was greater than the rest of the United States and, at less than three cents per acre, it was considered a bargain. It gave the new country almost all of America west of the Mississippi River.

Jefferson was a respected scientist who had long tried to finance overland exploration to the Pacific Ocean. He hoped to find the fabled Northwest Passage, although his interests were chiefly mapping and exploration. He persuaded Congress to finance an expedition and chose Captain Meriwether Lewis, his personal secretary, as leader. Lewis invited his friend, William Clark, as co-leader. They were charged *'to explore the Missouri River, and such principal stream of it, as, by its course and communication with the waters of the Pacific Ocean ... may offer the most direct and practicable water communication across this continent for the purpose of commerce'.*

Their journey began officially just beyond St Charles, Missouri (where the Missouri River flows into the Mississippi north of St Louis) on 14 May 1804 and ended in St Louis in September 1806. The first European explorers to cross the continent, they were able to gather important information about the Native peoples and the topography, flora and fauna of the vast region during their travels. Clark was an excellent mapmaker, and his cartographical work was invaluable. However, it was the expedition's rather poor treatment of Indian peoples that was to resonate throughout the century. Charles McKenzie, already noted for his pro-Indian views, sheds some light on the diplomatic skills of Lewis and Clark in his journals.

The First Expedition – AUTUMN 1804

In McKenzie's account of his first expedition he recalls his initial meeting with the members of the Lewis and Clark party who had built a small fort near the Mandan Indian settlement:

> *Here, we also found a party of forty Americains [sic] under the command of Captains Lewis and Clarke [sic], exploring a passage by the Missouri to the Pacific Ocean. They came up the river in a boat of twenty oars, accompanied by two pirogues. Their fortifications for winter quarters were nearly complete. They had held a council with the Mandanes and distributed many presents, but most of the chiefs did not accept of any from them.*

McKenzie then hears Lewis's account of the poor hospitality his party experienced at the hands of the Mandans. Characteristically McKenzie makes a point of talking to the Indians and not taking the word of the aggrieved Europeans under Lewis. He quotes a Mandan chief:

> *Had these Whites come amongst us with charitable views they would have loaded the Great Boat with necessities. It is true they have ammunition, but they prefer throwing it away idly than sparing a shot of it to a poor Mandan. Had I encountered these White warriors in the upper plains, my young men on horseback would soon do for them as they would do for so many wolves, for there are only two sensible men among them, the worker of iron and the mender of guns.*

Before leaving the Mandan camp, McKenzie pays the American expedition a final visit:

> *We lived contentedly and became intimate with the gentlemen of the American expedition, who on all occasions seemed happy to see us, and always treated us with civility and kindness. It is true, Captain Lewis could not make himself agreeable to us. He could speak fluently and learnedly on all subjects, but his inveterate disposition against the British stained, at least in our eyes, all his eloquence. Captain Clarke was equally well informed, but his conversation was always pleasant, for he seemed to dislike giving offence unnecessarily. The Missouri was free of ice the second of April, then the American gentlemen sent off their twenty oar boat, with ten men, for the United States, and on the 8th following, the expedition proceeded up the river towards the Rocky Mountains. It consisted of one large pirogue and seven small wooden canoes, containing the commanding officers, thirty men and a woman.*

The woman was Sacajawea ('Bird Woman'), a Shoshone interpreter whose local knowledge was to prove invaluable to the expedition. McKenzie did not mention her baby son, however, born in February in the winter camp, who was to survive the epic journey to the Pacific.

Comparison of the Lewis and Clark journals with McKenzie's lesser-known accounts shows that the Scot's observations were fairly accurate. His tally of the expedition does not differ much from the Americans' version and in his descriptions of native customs, wildlife and landscape the younger and less experienced McKenzie acquits himself very well. In turn it appears from Clark's accounts that he had a great respect for

Charles McKenzie and mentions him in his complete journals. Even the normally recalcitrant Lewis alludes to the Scot: '9th February, 1805. This morning fair and pleasant. Wind from the Southeast. Visited by Mr. McKenzie, one of the N.W. Company's clerks ....'

McKenzie's accounts of this time are confident, the writings of a young man revelling in adventure and danger. Lewis and Clark conveyed their experiences in a more formal tone, even when revealing the terrible problems that they (and McKenzie) encountered: 45 below zero weather, rheumatism, boils, toothache, abscesses, pleurisy (treated by blood-letting and sweating), sprains and dislocations. Sacajawea, for example, was said to have been assisted through childbirth by dissolving snake rattles in a glass of water.

Clark's journal entry for 29 March 1805 begs comparison with McKenzie's on the same subject. Says Clark:

The ice has stopped running, owing to some obstacle above. Repaired the boat and pirogues, and preparing to set out. But few Indians visited us today. They are now attending on the river bank to catch the floating buffalo. The obstacle broke away above, and the ice came down in great quantities. The river rose 13 inches in the last 24 hours. I observed extraordinary dexterity of the Indians in jumping from one cake of ice to another, for the purpose of catching the buffalo as they float down. Many of the cakes of ice which they pass over are not two feet square.

McKenzie consistently demonstrates his own fine attention to detail. Like Clark he speaks of the Mandan preference for drowned buffalo carcasses, and for swimming (even in winter):

Buffaloes and other animals are in immense numbers destroyed every winter by the Missouri Indians. In stormy weather, whole droves run from the mountains and plain to seek shelter in the woods which form the margin of the Missouri; many of them, attempting to cross when the ice is weak, sink and are drowned, and, in the spring both sides of the river are in several places covered with rotten carcasses and skeletons of buffaloes, elks, etc. These dead animals which often float down the current among the ice for hundreds of miles, are preferred by the natives to any other kind of food. When the skin is raised you will see the flesh of a greenish hue and ready to become alive at the least exposure to the sun and so ripe and tender that very little boiling is required. The stench is absolutely intolerable, yet the soup made from it, which becomes bottle green, is reckoned delicious. So fond are the Mandanes of putrid meat that they bury animals whole in the winter for consumption in the spring …. I had the opportunity of observing the courage and dexterity of the young Mandanes among the floating ice, hauling ashore some scores of these nauseous carcasses. The Mandanes are excellent swimmers; I was no less surprised to see in the drift ice the men occasionally leap from one block to another, often falling between, plunging under, darting up elsewhere and securing themselves upon very slippery flakes; yet no serious accident happened. The women performed their part equally well; you would see them slip out of their leather smoks, despising danger, plunge into the troubled deep to secure their object. The men and women of this place do not think it necessary to sew fig leaves together to make themselves aprons, and they are not ashamed to appear naked in public.

McKenzie's account, free from formality, is far more detailed than the Lewis and Clark treatment of the same subject, adhering to the writing adage of 'show not tell'. He comments on crops such as beans, corn and sunflowers, including a seed concoction which warriors ate while on the move. He also notes the taboo against women touching the sacred plant tobacco, save for preparing the ground for it. McKenzie thus finishes his account of the first expedition, commenting finally that it was chance encounters with the Rocky Mountain Indians that gave European traders the vital information that the valuable beaver was a common animal in the mountains.

The Second Expedition – JUNE 1805

McKenzie began his second expedition to the Upper Missouri in June 1805. He delights in the sight of some western Indians who arrive in the camp, and describes their dress and ornament, concluding 'they are the best riders in the world'. He realised later that he was talking about the Crows or *Corbeaux* (McKenzie uses the French word), whom he describes in great physical detail:

The men of the Corbeaux nation are generally of the middle size … with fair complexion and a pleasant countenance. The women are handsome, but their beauty fades early; even children have grey hairs. The women are careless about their hair which scarcely reaches the shoulders; to make it look fine they sometimes throw a little water over it.

Winfred Blevins noted in his book *Give Your Heart to the Hawks*:

> *The Crow people and Crow country were remarkable. The Crow men were tall, hand-*
> *some and statuesque; the women were handsome rather than beautiful .... Men and*
> *women alike had a keen, ribald sense of fun; Crows were the practical jokers of the*
> *mountains. Babies were strapped onto horses before they could walk, so all Crows were*
> *superb horsemen.* (page 54)

He also recounts a legend concerning the origins of the tribe, and lists some sample sentences to illustrate the differences between Gros Ventre and Corbeaux, adding that the Crows cannot pronounce the letter 'v' properly. McKenzie notes further details:

> *All these tribes dress in the same manner; the men have long hair which trails to the*
> *ground but to make it appear long they add horse hair by a cement of gum. The Corbeaux*
> *do not cut off joints of their fingers, nor slash their own flesh as the Gros Ventres do.*

When McKenzie leaves the camp he talks of meadows so full of buffalo that progress is impossible, and describes the torment of clouds of blood-sucking flies. The men almost die of thirst but arrive successfully back at Fort Assiniboine. The fort, under the command of one Major Henry, had run out of provisions due to a combination of bad weather and poor hunting. McKenzie's men, however, arrived with an abundance of food and they were able to alleviate starvation.

McKenzie supplemented his second expedition journal with a further account of an elaborate Festival of the Sun in the Enasa village on 10 July 1805. Several young braves made sacrifices by slicing off a finger or giving strips of flesh from their own bodies. Some of the devotees were suspended from the lodge roof by means of cords fastened through their shoulder blades. McKenzie appears sickened by the graphic scenes, but regardless of his own feelings took the trouble to unravel some of the mysteries surrounding tribal protocol. He also uses the occasion to illustrate Indian generosity. McKenzie was one of the first to observe the sacred notion of hospitality among the western tribes. The Enasas extended hospitality even to their enemies and guaranteed the safety of any individuals seeking refuge in their village. The extent of their tolerance in some cases was legendary.

The Third Expedition – AUGUST 1805

McKenzie returned to Upper Missouri with a small group and witnessed the return of a war party of Mandans who been involved in a battle with the Sioux. He could not sleep for the celebrations, and recounts a gruesome incident of the decapitation of a runaway slave woman (who had been intended as a present for him).

He also describes a buffalo hunt in winter, in which the animals were driven into an ice-swollen river, drowned, and left to float in a refrigerated state until their flesh was needed. McKenzie also recounts his own misfortunes: stolen horses, exposure to cold and near-starvation. Nonetheless, he seems pleased: 'When my returns were examined and the horses were recovered, my expedition was thought more of and, in the end, I had no reason to complain.'

THE FOURTH EXPEDITION – JUNE 1806

This was McKenzie's last expedition to Upper Missouri, his employers deciding that these trips were no longer profitable.

Arriving at the camp he discovered over 130 Indians had died from whooping cough. The people, despite their obvious distress, nevertheless found the strength of mind to celebrate the return of a war party.

Intrigued by the seeming inappropriateness of their behaviour, McKenzie meditates upon the native character in general. In this passage he is almost satirical in his description of how an Indian man is a true lord in his own tent:

He no sooner appears but everyone hurries to clear his way lest his feet should be entangled on his entering; every work is abandoned, every appearance of mirth disappears, no one dares salute him or even look at him in the face. After having put by his weapons, he will seat himself on his hams before a blazing fire with a great composure and air of dignity. The most slavish of his women (they have in general more than one) will approach him and take off his shoes and leggings, while another brings him water to drink and a third prepares his meal, which he devours without saying a word .... My Lord being now satiated and his first pipe smoked nearly to the bottom, he will, in a solemn and low tone, begin to relate the adventures of the day. He never thinks of blaming himself for his bad success.

McKenzie was witness to a visit by a band of Cheyennes, most of whom had never observed a European man before. He became an object of curiosity yet respect. 'All strangers treated me with the greatest kindness,' he comments. McKenzie was then pressed to return with the Cheyennes, who promised him that their own country abounded in precious beaver. The Mandans on the other hand believed that Europeans could not possibly be sane, seeking an animal that had no real value as far as they were concerned.

McKenzie ends one part of his account with this rather droll observation of a pipe ceremony between a European trader called Gissom and various tribal chieftains from the Cheyenne and Mandan nations. In this ceremony each man tries to intimidate and impress the others with philosophy, religion, bombast and boasting. McKenzie admitted that he 'was obliged to leave the fireside for laughter':

> Rattle Snake [a Cheyenne] and Mr. Gissom each took their pipe and filled it with all the ceremonies which superstition could invent, then cutting a branch of choke cherry and passing it through a piece of fat dried meat, they planted it into the ground close to each pipe .... Rattle Snake burst out in a kind of lamentation which lasted a quarter of an hour, and was chorused at the end by the others in a heavy murmur, as thanksgiving. Rattle Snake gave his pipe to a lad who sat alongside of him, who, after simulating to make the four elements smoke, without even lighting the pipe, made a hearty harangue in which he mentioned all the feats the Rattle Snake had accomplished, and implored the pity and assistance of all the living animals, fowls and insects.

McKenzie was most obviously touched by the hospitality he received from the Cheyennes and concluded that 'these six days I past with the greatest pleasure that Savage life could afford ....'

Receiving a visit at this time from three leading traders – Charles Chaboillez, Alexander Henry and Allen MacDonel – McKenzie was reproached for going native in dress and manner. He enjoyed the last laugh, however, for the Indians made it obvious that they were thoroughly disappointed in the mediocrity of the three men, expecting the great chiefs of the white people to be more gracious in their manner and regal in their appearance. McKenzie too expressed his disappointment at the ignorant manners of his 'superiors', giving the reader an insight into why he was never popular with his bosses.

In Upper Missouri, McKenzie described, almost poetically, the sights, smells and confusion of horses, men, dogs and camp followers, making up the vast procession of the entire Mandan and Gros Ventre camp, reaching almost two thousand horsemen. He notes: 'The Indians were dressed in their best and marched out flying colours and singing Indian songs ... weapons consisted of bow and arrows, lances, battleaxes, shields ....' Pandemonium, however, almost broke out when the Gros Ventre, Cheyenne and Mandan all threatened war against one another over a fairly minor misunderstanding involving unkept, or misunderstood, promises over the trading of horses and goods.

McKenzie's last words sum up his experience: 'I was not a little proud when I considered that I was the first North trader who crossed the Missouri with four packs of beaver.'

* * *

Charles McKenzie – *A Summary*

The opinions and observations of Charles McKenzie on the indigenous peoples of Canada are stated in the numerous journals and reports he submitted while in charge of an isolated and relatively unproductive post at Lac Seul, in what is now northwestern Ontario. His recurrent theme is the special relationship between Scots and First Nations people and he repeatedly criticises his employers for their mercantile treatment of the locals. His journals and letters express his view that the British government (and Hudson's Bay) were concerned with Indian people only for the sake of profit. In an article, 'Charles McKenzie, l'homme seul' by Elizabeth Arthur in *Ontario History* (volume LXX, 1978), the author argues that McKenzie had begun his travels with the interests of the Indian people at heart, but had changed his views radically over years of interaction:

> *There is no reason to believe that McKenzie, when he first came to North America, viewed the Indians any differently from other young Scots in the fur trade. In the early years the references he made to Indians in his journals were similar to those found in many contemporary accounts. The best-known Indians might receive a half-mocking description; the effect of policy upon the amount of fur to be collected was constantly*

noted in business-like fashion. But at this stage it was always a member of another civilisation holding himself aloof, noting what to him were outlandish customs. Gradually, however, this changed. The experience of isolation from his European inheritance, his study of the customs of the Indians around him, his devotion to his half-Scottish, half-Indian wife, Mary McKay, and his concern over the prejudice his children faced, created in McKenzie a set of ideas so remote from those of the early Victorian era that they merit some examination.

Although McKenzie resigned from the company in 1823, he returned in 1827 after living for a time in Montreal. However, it became apparent by 1830 that McKenzie would never achieve promotion. Sir George Simpson stated simply that 'his best days [were] gone'. Understandably McKenzie grew bitter and became increasingly outspoken in his views about his employers, often siding with Indian attitudes and customs rather than dismissing them as 'heathen' or 'barbaric', as was the custom of other writers. Elizabeth Arthur notes that he repeatedly protests about the treatment of individuals by the company. In 1847 McKenzie argued about the treatment of Metis (part French, part Native) canoe-maker who had fallen on hard times due to the indifference of his employer. The man, Baptiste Vincent, had 'put not a few thousand pounds into the Company's pockets in his Generation,' McKenzie noted sarcastically.

Elizabeth Arthur studied the Lac Seul journals in great detail and found them studded with pro-Indian references. McKenzie particularly found the company policy of hiring Natives and Metis for less desirable employment distasteful. Yet the company continued to hire Orcadians and Shetlanders for jobs that McKenzie felt could be done better by local people.

It is also significant that the three Scots central to this book married native women and were concerned about the plight of their own mixed-blood children, whom they believed suffered from intense bigotry. McKenzie felt that his children would have more opportunity outwith Hudson's. His son, Hector Aeneas, was clearly treated as subservient by the company because of his mixed race, and was only permitted to occupy the post of postmaster at a lesser pay, with few prospects of promotion.

But McKenzie's attitudes were too radical for the company and for his contempories. If his ideas on the equality of Native peoples worked against his promotion within the fur-trading industry, his attitude toward his wife, and towards women in a man's world in general, were just as controversial. Hudson's had a strict men-only policy and women were tolerated only in so far as they served the men of the company, often as 'wives' after the custom of the country.

There were exceptions, however, like Isabella Gunn of Orkney and Letitia MacTavish of Campbeltown. Isabella, born in Orkney in 1788, disguised herself as a man called John Fubister and enlisted with Hudson's Bay where she served with distinction for three years. She risked starvation and drowning, and once canoed over 1800 miles through the northern wilderness. Isabella's secret identity was finally discovered when she gave birth to a baby boy. However, policy was policy, and this brave trapper and explorer who had, in the language of the male trappers, 'worked at any thing, and well, like the rest of the men', was put to work washing the men's laundry until she could be shipped back to Orkney. There she died in poverty and disgrace and was buried in a pauper's grave in Kirkwall.

Letitia MacTavish further illustrates the treatment of women in the fur-trading industry. MacTavish grew up near Campbeltown where many of the men in her family had connections with the Canadian fur trade. Her husband was a chief trader at York Factory, where she joined him as the only white woman seen in those parts. Her letters to her family in Scotland detailed the harsh life in the trading post and were particularly sympathetic towards Native women, who called her *Hockimaw Erqua* ('Woman Chief'). She often clashed with local ministers and educators about their attitudes towards local women and their misunderstanding of native customs and ways, and was considered an embarrassment to the company. But her written accounts provide rare insight and are thought to be some of the first writings by a woman in Canada. Letitia returned to Scotland for medical treatment in 1846, but died of cholera in Sault St Marie (in present-day Ontario) in 1854.

McKenzie encouraged his wife to hunt and to pursue her own customs, and never referred to her as a squaw but as 'the guid wife' or 'my better half'. He appeared pleased with his wife's abilities and often defended her spirited and independent attitude against the company.

His daughter Catherine married a mixed-blood trapper, Thomas Cook, and again McKenzie created a stir among his contemporaries when he defended any young woman's decision to marry a man without parental intervention, not the done thing in colonial Canada.

* * *

Elizabeth Arthur concludes her article 'Charles McKenzie, l'homme seul':

> *In the study of the impressive business success of the Hudson's Bay Company under*
> *Simpson's leadership, it is necessary to see at what cost in human terms that this*
> *success was achieved. It is necessary to examine the failure, the obverse side of the*
> *medal, and this McKenzie's records permit us to do. In his journals appear the results*
> *of Company policy, however advantageous that policy may have been, upon a*
> *particular area – an area which sprang into prominence because of the rivalry of fur*
> *trading companies at the beginning of the nineteenth century, and an area which, once*
> *that rivalry ceased, was left to its fat, in callous disregard of the irreversible effects*
> *upon the native people that a generation of the fur trade had produced.*

In 1842 McKenzie gave Roderick MacKenzie a manuscript that detailed his four Missouri expeditions. From this account, L R Masson, grandson-in-law of Roderick MacKenzie, published a *Narrative of Four Trading Expeditions to the Missouri* (Les Bourgeois de la Compagnie du Nord-Ouest, 1889). In it he noted: 'Mr. McKenzie has a most decided partiality for the Indians, of whom, on all occasions, he made himself the apologist ....'

Referring to the Indians, Masson quotes McKenzie:

> *Nay they are more degraded and degenerated than when the first European set his foot*
> *on American soil, the epoch of the setting Sun of its native inhabitants. There is every*
> *appearance of the quick extinction of the North American Indians, but no distant hope*
> *of improving their mind. They think that being, as they say, under the protection of the*
> *British Government is enough. What, in the name of Goodness, is that protection the*
> *British Government ever afforded the natives of this country? Has not the British*
> *Government sold them to a monopoly?*

Although the word had not yet been coined, 'genocide' was what McKenzie was referring to. His journals and records, though never widely circulated, brought into question the actions of the profit-motivated businesses of the time, and their devastating effect on the Native peoples who had earned McKenzie's respect from his earliest days on the Missouri River, smoking the pipe of peace with Mandan, Gros Ventre and Cheyenne.

Appendix I
A Select List
of Tribes

THIS list is not meant to be comprehensive. It includes the names of tribes encountered by Scots from the Canadian arctic to the Florida swamps and southwestern deserts. Scots explored and settled virtually all the territories of North America and most of the tribes listed here were part of the Scottish experience.

Reid, Ross and McKenzie had strong cultural contact with only a handful of tribes, although the latter two were traders who encountered Native peoples including Crow, Blackfeet, Assiniboine, Cree, Okanagan, and many others. Without special knowledge it is easy to confuse the Crow with the Creek or Cree, or various bands of Sioux (Lakota) and Apache, as well as alternative names like Ojibway (Canadian) or Chippewa (American). This short list is designed to assist the general reader.

Apache: A southwest tribe, from a Zuni word meaning 'Enemy'. The Apache called themselves *Dine*, 'the People', and were renowned warriors. There were six principal Apache groups – the Jicarillas, Kiowa, Lipans, Mescaleros, Chiricahuas and the Coyotero. Geronimo and Cochise were probably two of the best-known Apaches.

Arapaho: A hunting culture from the Great Plains. The Arapaho came originally from the Great Lakes, but ended up in Colorado and Wyoming. They were allied with the Cheyenne and fought alongside other tribes in the Plains Wars of the 1870s. They now live in Oklahoma and Wyoming.

Assiniboine: A hunting, nomadic tribe living on the Border with Canada and found mainly in Montana and Saskatchewan. They openly traded with Europeans, but their contact with traders and trappers brought increased susceptibility to smallpox and other diseases.

Blackfeet: By the time of European contact the Blackfeet were a nomadic hunting culture in the Northern Plains and Rocky Mountains. The main divisions were the Piegans, Siksika and Bloods. They were proud warriors whose chief enemies were the Crows. They fought bitterly against all white people who entered their tribal lands. The tribe was ravaged by smallpox in the 1830s. The Blackfeet were so-called because of the colour of the leather they used for moccasins.

Cherokee: One of the 'Five Civilised Tribes' (with the Creek, Choctaw, Chickasaw and Seminole) because of their use of a written alphabet and constitution. (This title came about from early European traders who noted that these people had many similarities with white social structures.) The Cherokee, in early contact with these traders and explorers, were first to suffer from related epidemics. They were native to modern-day Georgia, which had a huge Scottish population including many Gaelic-speaking Highlanders. The Cherokee were forcibly moved to western reservations in a long march known as 'The Trail of Tears'. Many died on that march. The Cherokee now live mainly in Oklahoma, although some remain in Carolina. Sequoyah, a Cherokee scholar, is credited with the invention of an 86-syllable phonetic alphabet to enable his people to read and write.

Cheyenne: A nomadic, buffalo-hunting tribe of the plains. *Cheyanne* is a Dakota name for 'People of a Different Speech'. Their own name, *Tsistsistas*, means 'the People'. The Cheyenne were pressured from their eastern home-lands by the Dakotas. Known particularly for their spiritual symbols and talismans, they too suffered greatly from disease and were victims of the infamous Sand Creek massacre in 1864. The Cheyenne split into northern and southern factions and the former played a major role in General Custer's defeat at Little Bighorn on 25 June 1876. The tribe is now split between Oklahoma and Montana. They were also famed for their resistance to reservations. In 1878 several hundred Cheyenne fled their reservation for their ancestral homeland in the Powder River and won the right, through battle and perseverance, to live there.

Chickasaw: A tribe native to Mississippi. They fought with the South during the American Civil War. They had very early contact with Spanish explorers and, like the other 'Civilised' tribes, adopted many European customs including reading and writing. They also suffered from common diseases brought in by Europeans, including measles and smallpox. Like the Cherokee, they were forcibly removed to reservations in what is now Oklahoma.

Chinook: A Columbia River tribe who were primarily salmon fishers. Their language was simplified for use as a trade language among many other tribes in the Pacific northwest.

Chipewyan: Indians of Athabascan stock, native to northwest Canada. Well known to traders and fur trappers in what is now Saskatchewan and Alberta.

Chippewa: An American form of Ojibway (Canadian) – (*see* **Ojibway**).

Clatsop: A Pacific northwest tribe along the Columbia River in what is now Oregon and Washington state.

Comanche: Also spelt 'Camanche' and 'Cumanche'. A Shoshonean tribe who lived in what is now Colorado. They were considered the best horsemen on the Great Plains, making them formidable warriors and hunters of buffalo. The Comanche protected their lands from settlers and other tribes alike, driving the Apache further south. They suffered from smallpox and cholera, but it was the destruction of the great buffalo herds on the Southern Plains in the 1870s that sealed their fate as nomadic hunters. They adopted the peyote cult from Mexico in 1879. This was based on hallucinogenic use of peyote buttons (discs) from the southwest cactus (*Lophophora williamsi*), eaten ceremoniously to aid meditation, prayers and visions. The name is taken from the Aztec *peyotl*. Unlike other tribes, the Comanche received individual land grants instead of tribal reservations. Many historians, soldiers and other Indians considered the Comanche the finest fighters on the plains.

Cree (Eenou): A tribe of Algonquin stock, based mainly in what is now Manitoba, Canada, although their historical range was once more extensive. The Cree traded primarily with the Hudson's Bay Company, playing an important part in its history. The Cree had particularly strong ties with Orkney and Orcadians. Flett, a common Orkney name, is also common among the Cree. They are renowned as hunters and trappers and still play an integral role in the Canadian fur trade.

Creek: A southern American tribe whose chiefs included names like McGillivray and McIntosh. One of the 'Five Civilised Tribes' who lived in the lands know known as Georgia and Alabama. They became the dominant tribe of the 'Five' and adopted many European customs; but they were also very independent in their tribal dealings with the French, Spanish, British and Americans. The tribe fought on both sides during the Civil War and were forced to cede tribal lands to the victors. They were involuntarily removed to western lands where they allied with other tribes. They tried to enter the American Union as an Indian state, almost successfully, but instead merged their lands with the state of Oklahoma which was admitted to the Union in 1907.

Crow (French *Corbeaux*): A buffalo-hunting tribe from the Great Plains and Rocky Mountain area. Their own name is *Absaroka*, meaning 'Children of the Mountain Raven'. They lived along the southern tributaries of the Yellowstone River in what is now Wyoming and Montana. Their traditional enemies were the Blackfeet, Lakota and Shoshone. The Crow were fond of horses and amenable to trading with Europeans. They were probably the favourite tribe of American trappers and traders, often serving as scouts for the US army. The Crow now live along the Little Bighorn River.

Delaware: Algonquin Indians who lived along the eastern seaboard. They were one of the first tribes encountered by Scots. They called themselves *Lenni-Lenape* ('Real Men'). They were pushed westwards and settled in what is now Ohio. Some joined with Europeans in the Rocky Mountain fur trade. Many now live in Oklahoma.

Flathead: A Salish tribe living in Western Montana. The tribe did not actually flatten their heads as some tribes did, although they flattened the heads of slaves and captives. The name is probably taken from their sign language: the common signage for the tribe was two hands laid flat against the side of the signee's head. Flathead Indians traded freely with Europeans. They still live in northern Montana.

Gros Ventre: The Gros Ventre of the Missouri (the *Hidatsa*), neighbours of the Mandans, were the Indians Charles McKenzie met on his expeditions to the Missouri Country. These Gros Ventre should not be confused with the Gros Ventre of the Prairie, the *Atsina* of the northern prairies of Montana and southern Canada. The northern Gros Ventre were considered Blackfeet by Europeans because they were so closely allied with the Blackfeet tribe.

Huron: An eastern tribe of the Iroquois family. They were great practitioners of lacrosse, considered a curative game by the tribe.

Iroquois: A large confederation of eastern tribes, probably the most important such grouping, including Seneca, Mohawk, Oneida, Cayuga, Huron and

Onondaga, with various sub-groupings as well. Scots met the Iroquois first in New York State and in eastern Canada. Many Iroquois worked in the fur trade alongside the French and Scots, and some went west with the expansion of the fur companies. Alexander Ross writes about some of the Iroquois who went on fur-gathering expeditions with him.

Lakota: Popularly known as the Sioux. *Lakota* is a variant of *Dakota* and *Nakota*. The Teton Sioux called themselves *Lakota* and this name seems to be the most acceptable for the Sioux as a whole. The Teton Sioux included such well known individuals as Sitting Bull, Crazy Horse and Red Cloud. The word *Sioux* itself probably comes from a shortened Ojibway word for 'Enemy'. *Dakota* means 'an Alliance of Friends'. They often referred to their tribes as 'the Seven Council Fires'. The Lakota left their first home on the Great Lakes and gradually settled in the western prairies. Some of the seven tribes were farmers, not nomads. All the tribes had elaborate religions involving visions, the sun dance, and the Ghost Dance, which was to herald a new era when buffalo would return and white people would leave the land to the Indians. The Lakota were instrumental in the wars against US troops, and played a major part in the victory at the Little Bighorn. Some fled to Canada, others took up the Ghost Dance which culminated in the Massacre at Wounded Knee in 1890. The Lakota now live in North and South Dakota and Nebraska. The tribes of this nation evoke popular images of the Plains Indian and their culture and religion – *ie* movie images, familiar depictions of horses, bows and arrows, *etc*. They had long associations with the Badlands and the Black Hills. The Lakota have also been at the centre of a revival of pride in Indian culture, customs and language.

Mandan: A Siouan tribe living along the upper reaches of the Missouri River in what is now North Dakota. This tribe was in early contact with European trappers and explorers, including the Lewis and Clark Expedition. Charles McKenzie stayed with them during his four expeditions to the Upper Missouri. They were a hunting and farming society and were skilled potters. McKenzie observed their religious ceremonies. There was a theory that the Mandan were an offshoot of early Welsh settlers and there have been many attempts made to link the Welsh and Mandan languages. The tribe was almost entirely wiped out by smallpox in 1837.

Metis: The Metis (pronounced '*May*-tee') were of mixed-blood descent from Europeans and local Indians. Mainly French-speaking, they were an important cultural and political influence around the Red River Colony. They rose in armed rebellion in 1885. Their leaders, Luis Riel and Gabriel Dumont, have become Canadian icons. The Metis were vital to the fur trade and a crucial link in relations between Europeans and Indians. Although predominately French-Indian, some Metis were also of Scots descent. The Spanish term *mestizo* for people of mixed blood is similar, both derived from Latin.

Mohawk: One of the eastern tribes of the Iroquois Confederacy, centred principally in what is now New York State. A tribe well known to Lachlan Campbell's Highland settlement there in the eighteenth century.

Nez Perce: A northwest tribe, in what is now Idaho. They changed from a salmon-fishing to a hunting culture when they mastered the use of horses. They bred appaloosas. They gradually became more nomadic and crossed the mountains to hunt buffalo. The Nez Perce were initially friendly, but a gold rush resulted in pressures on their land and culture. This pressure resulted in the Nez Perce wars of 1877. The tribe was lead by Chief Joseph, whose honour and dignity became legendary. The name itself comes from French traders. However, although the tribe call themselves *Nimipu* ('Pierced Nose'), they did not adopt the practice. To add to the confusion, the tribe do not pronounce their name the French way but simply as 'Nez Purse', so this should be seen as the courteous rendition of the name. The Scots historian Dr James Hunter has detailed Scottish connections, through the McDonalds of Glencoe, to the Nez Perce tribe and the wars of 1877. Scottish fur trappers encountered the tribe and wrote extensively about them.

Ojibway (Chippewa): Tribe of the Great Lakes Region, Wisconsin in the USA and Ontario in Canada. The name is derived from the characteristic puckered seam on their moccasins. They call themselves *Anishinabe*, 'the First Men'. A woodland culture, they lived in *tipis* and gathered and farmed wild rice. The Ojibway were fur trappers and traders and sided with the French against the British and Americans. Many Scots in the trapping business learned their craft from them before going further west. The Ojibway were particularly adept at trapping beaver, an animal central to the fur economy and notoriously difficult to capture.

Osage: A Siouan tribe of the Southern Plains which included the Kansa, Omaha, Ponca and others. They farmed and hunted. The Osage lived in Missouri, Kansas and Illinois, but were gradually pushed west, completing their emigration from the Atlantic seaboard that began many centuries before. They were removed to reservations in the 1870s.

Pawnee: A confederacy of tribes in the Central Plains. The Pawnee were both nomadic and agricultural. The name means 'horn' and comes from the custom of twisting the forelocks of the men into long horns. They fought principally with the Lakota, Cheyenne and Arapaho and had very detailed religious ceremonies. They lived in what is now Nebraska, but were settled on reservations in Oklahoma. Many settlers first saw the Pawnee on the initial stage of their overland journey from Missouri into the Great Plains.

Sac- (Sauk-)Fox: Woodland tribe of the American midwest, chiefly Illinois, Iowa, Michigan and Wisconsin. The tribe engaged in hunting, trapping and agriculture. Possibly the most famous chief was Black Hawk who led his people in war in 1832. They fought valiantly but finally had to cede most of their lands. The remnants of the tribe lives in Iowa and Oklahoma.

Seminole: A renowned tribe, never subdued, who lived in the forests and swamps of Florida. One of the 'Five Civilised Tribes' who resisted European encroachment into their lands.

Shoshone ('Snake'): A widespread tribe living along the Rocky Mountains, from Idaho and Wyoming up into Alberta. The Shoshone Indians were also called the 'Snake' Indians by trappers and traders, especially the Scots. The name is thought to have come from a sign language misunderstanding of the word 'snake'. The Shoshone were said to have a very sinuous and graceful sign language.

The acquisition of horses meant the tribe could hunt buffalo and they became a more nomadic people, although other branches of the Shoshone lived primarily from salmon fishing. The famous interpreter Sacajawea was a Shoshone. The Shoshone and their great chief Washakie were generally peaceful towards Europeans, but naturally resented incursions through their country by settlers and by the Mormons. Many Shoshone women and children were killed in a massacre on Idaho's Bear River in 1863.

The name is pronounced 'Shoshonee', with the final 'e' elongated. As an adjective, the 'e' is often silent.

Sioux: (*see* Lakota)

Ute: The Utes were southwest Indians in what is now Colorado and Utah and were well-known to Scots traders, trappers and explorers. Originally hunter-gatherers, the horse radically changed their culture, but they rarely hunted buffalo, becoming renowned horsemen, and horse thieves, instead.

They won a court settlement against the American government concerning their original Colorado reservation, from which they were removed illegally for less desirable lands in Utah.

Yakima: A tribe that lived in what is now Oregon and Washington, along the Columbia and Yakima Rivers. They were originally salmon fishers but the horse enabled them to become hunters as well. They fought against incursions across their reservation. Federal dams destroyed many of their ancient fishing waters, for which they received compensation. They were also excellent horsemen.

Appendix II
Some other Scots in North America

Campbell, Robert (1808-94): From Glen Lyon, Perthshire, Campbell joined the Hudson's Bay Company in 1830. An extraordinary trapper and explorer, he once walked 3000 miles on snowshoes. During one adventure he saved his men from starvation by boiling his snowshoes into an edible paste. He was a source of wonder to Native peoples because he habitually took a morning dip in icy waters. Campbell's wife, Eleanor Stirling from Comrie, made a difficult 6000-mile journey to join her husband in the Canadian wilderness.

Cuming, Sir Alexander (1690-1775): From Culter, Aberdeenshire, Cuming went to the Cherokee country to collect herbs and minerals, but ended up persuading the locals to crown him 'Emperor of the Cherokee' and 'Crown King of Tennessee'. He returned to London with some of his Cherokee faithful to present to King George II. Cuming died a visionary pauper in Charterhouse, London.

Dickson, Robert (1765-1823): Originally from Dumfries, Dickson emigrated to Canada and became a fur trapper and trader near Lake Huron, where he married To-to-Win, the daughter of a great Sioux chief. Dickson had a vision of a great co-operative trading settlement and was appointed Indian Agent for all the tribes west of Lake Huron, where he was widely respected by the First Nations peoples of the area.

Dunbar, William (1749-1810): Dunbar came from Elgin, Morayshire. He emigrated to America in 1771, setting up as an Indian trader and merchant near Baton Rouge, Louisiana. His slaves revolted, however, and he had his land confiscated during the American Revolution. Dunbar made many scientific discoveries and carried out an important study of Native Indian sign languages.

Gunn, Isabella (1788-1861): Isabella Gunn was an Orkney woman who disguised herself as a man, John Fubister, in order to work for the men-only

Hudson's Bay. She was a successful trapper, canoeist and explorer until her ruse was discovered when she gave birth to a child. Despite her excellent work, she was deported to Scotland in disgrace. Back home she was teased and reviled as a single mother and witch, and at her death buried in a pauper's grave. It is certain that Isabella worked successfully among the First Nations peoples of Canada and her example highlights shortcomings in the fur trade, as far as the treatment of women was concerned.

Hall, Andy (1848-82): From Liddesdale, Andy Hall became an explorer, Indian fighter and lawman. He boasted that he grew his hair long to tempt would-be scalpers. He gained respect from the Apache, but was most famous for his key role in the expedition in 1869 of John Wesley Powell down the Colorado River, through the Grand Canyon.

MacDonald, Ranald (1824-94): Born in what is now Washington State, to an Argyll Highlander and local Indian named Princess Sunday. MacDonald had many incredible adventures, but is credited in particular with helping to open up Japan to foreign trade. He was a legend among his mother's people along the Kettle River.

McGillivray, Alexander (1759-93): Born in Alabama, McGillivray was the son of Lachlan McGillivray who came from Strathglass, and Sehoy Marchand, a half-French, half-Creek Indian. McGillivray became a chief and negotiated his tribe through some difficult times in their history. He was termed 'half Spaniard, half Frenchman, half Scot – all scoundrel' by his enemies, but he was also considered by one historian as 'the greatest Creek Indian chief who ever lived'.

McGregor, Thomas (1837-1910): From Paisley, McGregor went to New York City, then west to pan for gold. He joined the US cavalry and fought in the American Civil War where he was twice wounded. He saw action in various Indian wars in the west and was made Brigadier General in 1901. The Cheyenne and Apache had enormous respect for him.

McIntosh, William (1775-1825): MacIntosh was the son of a Scot and a Creek Indian woman. He tried to protect his people against British and American incursion, but in the end was shot dead by his own tribe because he had persuaded part of the tribe to sign a treaty with the US government, in defiance of the wishes of others.

Mackenzie, Donald (1783-1851): Mackenzie was from Ross-shire and gave his skills to various fur companies. He was a remarkable trapper, fighter, marksman and explorer. He was immortalised by the leading novelist of the time, Washington Irving, in his account of Astor's settlement, *Astoria*, where Mackenzie's considerable adventures are recounted. A huge man, by all accounts, he was nonetheless so agile that he was nicknamed 'Perpetual Motion'.

Mackenzie, Kenneth (1797-1861): Mackenzie was another Ross-shire man who began with the North West Company in Canada before making his fortune in the American trade. He opened up trading posts all over the west, where his penchant for fine food, women and wine earned him the titles of 'Emperor of the West' and 'King of the Missouri'. Mackenzie's reputation was mixed, but he was a colourful character who played a key role in the western fur trade, particularly in Blackfeet country.

Mackenzie, Ranald Slidell (1840-89): Mackenzie was born to Scottish parents in New York City. He fought in most of the bloodiest campaigns in the American Civil War on the Union side, and had several fingers shot off. He was known as 'Bad Hand' by the Indians. Mackenzie went west and fought against the Lakota, Cheyenne and Comanche. He was respected for his level-headed approach and fair treatment of enemies and captives.

MacLeod, James Farquharson (1836-94): Thought to have come from Glen Drynoch, in Skye, a cleared area, MacLeod's family grew up among the Ojibway in Ontario. He was the first Superintendent of the newly-formed Mounties. He was also an able diplomat with the Blackfeet and is famous for his fair treatment of Sitting Bull and his Lakota warriors who fled to Canada after the defeat of General Custer at Little Bighorn. MacLeod saved them from starving by supplying the warriors with food during their first harsh winter in Canada.

MacNeill, Andrew (*c.*1750-1820): The fictional character MacNeill (from Barra, via Glasgow) appears in the accounts of Hector St John de Crevecoeur about life in the New World (*Letters from an American Farmer*, in the chapter, 'What is an American?' The book was first published in 1782 and became an immediate hit in Europe.) He gives a graphic account of this Hebridean's first encounter with the Native peoples of Pennsylvania. Andrew may have been a fictional device for the French author, but is probably based on several real people.

MacTavish, Letitia (1813-54): MacTavish came from Campbeltown, Argyll. Many of her family had been involved in the Canadian fur trade. She became the wife of a chief trader with Hudson's Bay and showed great sympathy with local Indian women, sometimes clashing with educators and ministers over their treatment of the local people. Her accounts of everyday life, and of the Early Nations peoples, are invaluable to historians. She died of cholera.

Monroe (Munroe), Hugh (1798-1892): Born in Scotland, Monroe went west at age 16 and taught himself many Indian languages. He married into the Blackfeet tribe. He spent most of his life with the tribe, as trapper and trader, and died at Two Medicine River, Alberta, Canada in 1892.

Muir, Samuel (1789-1832): Muir was the son of the Reverend James Muir of Cumnock, Ayrshire. He studied medicine at the University of Edinburgh, and became an army surgeon. He married into the Sac-Fox tribe and became one of their leaders for over a decade. He died while fighting a cholera epidemic in Galena, Illinois.

Philip, James ('Scotty') (1858-1910): Philip came from Dallas, Morayshire and had many western adventures. He showed great insight into the plight of the Cheyenne and Lakota and was said to be the great warrior Crazy Horse's brother-in-law. Philip is credited with helping save the American buffalo from extinction by keeping pure herds for breeding. He was called 'The Buffalo King'.

Phillips, William Addison (1824-93): Originally from Paisley, Phillips emigrated to Illinois where he became a newspaper editor and lawyer. He went west to Kansas and did much to stop it from becoming a slave state. He commanded a regiment of American Indians during the Civil War. He was a socialist land reformer who fought for the rights of Indians and in particular fought in the courts for the land rights claims of the Cherokee tribe. He was also a poet and writer of fiction.

Rae, John (1813-93): Rae was an extraordinary man. Originally from Orkney, he was a surgeon with Hudson's Bay, but devoted much of his time to exploration and scientific study. Rae did much to narrow the search for Sir John Franklin in 1854. Franklin (1786-1847) was an explorer who went missing in the Canadian Arctic on his third voyage sometime during 1845-47. He and the entire crews of the ships *Erebus* and *Terror* were reported to have died from cold or starvation. His widow offered a huge reward for evidence of her husband's death, prompting many fruitless searches for their whereabouts. In 1854 Rae discovered physical evidence which allowed others to piece together the puzzle of Franklin's disappearance.

John Rae studied the Native tribes and adopted many of their ways, claiming that he learned much about survival and travel from them. Rae charted nearly 6000 miles of wilderness. He is buried in the churchyard of St Magnus Cathedral in Kirkwall, Orkney.

Ross, John (1790-1866): Ross was the son of a Scottish trader, David Ross, and Cherokee-Scottish mother named Mary MacDonald, whose forebears came from Inverness. His Indian name was *Kooseskowe* ('White Bird'). Ross was chief of the Cherokees for over 40 years and led the tribe at the time of the 'Trail of Tears' forced marches to Oklahoma reservations.

St Clair, Arthur (1736-1818): St Clair (Sinclair) came from a notable Caithness family, studying medicine at the University of Edinburgh before becoming a soldier in Colonial America. He fought for the Americans during the Revolution. He probably managed to avoid Indian massacre by trying to treat the Delaware and Shawnee tribes fairly, but was defeated in an important frontier battle by Little Turtle, on the Wabash River. St Clair was considered incompetent by the American frontiersmen who served under him and was judged inept by most historians. He died in poverty, writing a defence of his conduct of the Indian wars on the American frontier.

Stewart, Sir William Drummond (1795-1871): Stewart was born into a landed Perthshire family and grew up in Murthly Castle. He fought with honour at Waterloo, but his restless spirit took him to the American west where he lived the life of a frontiersman and fur trapper, albeit with as much luxury as he could afford. Stewart brought buffalo, Indians, scouts and trappers back to his castle. There is still a story in Dunkeld of a wagon full of fur trappers and Indians being pulled through the streets by buffalo. He relished his time among the Crow and Blackfeet and took a suit of armour west with him. Stewart wrote some fictional accounts of his adventures. He also made a fortune in railway investment. It is possible that Indian legends of the far west include this character who rode about in 'shining buckskin'.

Stobo, Richard (1724-85): Stobo came from Glasgow and went to Virginia as a tobacco merchant. He soldiered with George Washington, until he was captured by the French. He was recaptured and sentenced to death, but escaped again. Certainly Stobo had mishaps with the Indian allies of the French, but his real claim to fame is the character Lieutenant Lismahago, in the Tobias Smollett novel *Humphrey Clinker*. In that novel the fictional character marries a beautiful Indian woman and becomes chief of her tribe. He thus becomes 'Occaccanastaogarora', supposedly meaning 'nimble as a weasel'.

Stuart, John (1700-79): Stuart emigrated as a soldier at the age of 50. He fought against the Spanish in what is now Florida. His familiarity with the Cherokees resulted in his appointment as Superintendent for Indian Affairs, and he helped to negotiate treaties with the Cherokee, Creek and Catawba Indians. His work was interrupted by the American Revolution and he died in Pensacola, Florida

Stuart, Robert (1785-1848): Stuart hailed from Callander, Perthshire. He emigrated to Canada, working as a fisherman before becoming a fur trapper. Stuart had some epic adventures in the fur trade and was one of the first men to cross the North American continent by canoe. He became Superintendent for Indian Affairs for Michigan, owing much of his success to an understanding of Indian languages and customs.

Williamson, Peter ('Indian Peter') (1730-99): Kidnapped off the streets of Aberdeen at the age of ten, Williamson was sold into slavery in America, a common, lucrative practice. On gaining his freedom, he was held hostage by Indians who were allies of the French. He escaped and eventually returned to Aberdeen where he took out a court case against several prominent men who had become rich from the practice of kidnapping. Williamson settled in Edinburgh and established a coffee house called 'Indian Peter's'. He was a legendary character, calling himself 'King of the Mohawks'.

Bibliography

NOTE: These books are available in larger public libraries. Many are standard reference works which should be accessible in most large library collections in the United Kingdom.

Appleton's Cyclopaedia of American Biography (Wilson, New York).

Arthur, Elizabeth: 'Charles McKenzie, l'homme seul' in *Ontario History* (Toronto, 1978), vol. LXX, pp 39-61.

Black, George Fraser: *Scotland's Mark on America* (New York, 1921).

Blevins, Winfred: *Give Your Heart to the Hawks: A Tribute to the Mountain Men* (Avon, New York, 1976).

Blevins, Winfred (compiler): *The Wordsworth Dictionary of the American West: a panorama of Wild West fact and fiction* (Wordsworth Editions: Ware, Herts, 1995).

Brander, Michael: *The Emigrant Scots* (1982).

Bryan, Tom: *Rich Man, Beggar Man, Indian Chief: Fascinating Scots in Canada and America* (Thistle Press: Aberdeenshire, 1997).

Bumstead, J M: *The Scots in Canada* (1982).

Bunyan, Ian (*et al*): *No Ordinary Journey: John Rae, Arctic Explorer 1813-1893* (National Museums of Scotland: Edinburgh, 1993).

Dakin, Susanna Bryant: *A Scotch Paisano: Hugo Reid's Life in California, 1832-1852 Derived from His Correspondence* (University of California Press: Berkeley, 1939).

Dictionary of Canadian Biography (1963).

Finley, John H: *The Coming of the Scot* (Scribner's: New York, 1940).

Hewitson, Jim: *Tam Blake and Company: The Story of the Scots in America* (Canongate: Edinburgh, 1993).

Hook, Andrew: *Scotland and America* (Blackie and Sons: 1975).

Hunter, James: *Glencoe and the Indians* (Mainstream: Edinburgh, 1996).

Lewis, Jon E: *The West: The Making of the American West* (Siena: Bristol, 1998).

McKenzie, Charles: 'The Missouri Indians: A Narrative of Four Trading Expeditions to the Missouri: 1804-1805-1806', for the North West Company (see Masson, L R below).

Martin, Ged and Simpson: *Jeffrey Canada's Heritage in Scotland* (Dundurn Press: Toronto, 1989).

Masson, L R: *A Narrative of Four Trading Expeditions to the Missouri* (Les Bourgeois de la Compagnie du Nord-Ouest, 1889), vol. I, pp 327-93.

Porter, Mae Reed and Odessa Davenport: *Scotsman in Buckskin: Sir William Drummond Stewart and the Rocky Mountain Fur Trade* (Hastings House: New York, 1963).

Reid, W Stanford: *The Scottish Tradition in Canada* (1976).

Ross, Alexander: *Adventures of the First Settlers on the Oregon or Columbia River: being a narrative of the expedition fitted out by John Jacob Astor to establish the 'Pacific Fur Company'; with an account of some Indian Tribes on the coast of the Pacific, by Alexander Ross, one of the adventurers* (Smith, Elder and Co: London, 1849).

Ross, Alexander: *The Fur Hunters of the Far West: a narrative of adventures in the Oregon and Rocky Mountains in two volumes* (Smith, Elder and Co: London, 1855), 2 vols.

Ross, Alexander: *The Red River Settlement* (Smith, Elder and Co: London, 1849).

Ross, Peter: *The Scot in America* (1927).

Caveat: Most historians know that journals and diaries can often be amended, bowdlerised and censored over their long course of survival and publication. This explains certain inconsistencies, inaccuracies or abrupt changes of style or points of view. Of course the writer also has vested interests in self-promotion. Further, society's expectations might have forced the writer into safer conclusions. Traces of this might be seen in Alexander Ross, but Charles McKenzie, often critical of his employers, seems to have escaped mainly with replies or rebuttals written in the margins of his log books. It is likely that many of his criticisms would not have remained had his employers known that his writings would be published many years later.

It is probably safe to conclude that all three writers' views are openly represented and have survived with textual integrity. Their observations on Native American cultures are mainly accurate and judicious, and hence of value to readers today.